D1132884
Potsdam
Sept 8, 1961

*Folger Documents of Tudor and Stuart Civilization*

# AN APOLOGY OF THE CHURCH OF ENGLAND

## FOLGER DOCUMENTS
## OF TUDOR AND STUART CIVILIZATION

THIS volume is one of a series of publications of Tudor and Stuart documents that the Folger Library proposes to bring out. These documents will consist of hitherto unprinted manuscripts as well as reprints of rare books in the Folger Library. An effort will be made to choose significant items that will throw light on the social and intellectual background of the period from 1485 to 1715. In response to almost unanimous requests of interested historians, the spelling, punctuation, and capitalization will be modernized in printed texts. In some cases, where the original printing is clear and easily read, texts may be photographically reproduced. The Folger Library is prepared to supply microfilm of original texts to scholars who require a facsimile.

THE FOLGER SHAKESPEARE LIBRARY IS ADMINISTERED
BY THE TRUSTEES OF AMHERST COLLEGE.

# AN APOLOGY OF THE CHURCH OF ENGLAND

BY JOHN JEWEL

EDITED BY

*J. E. Booty*

PUBLISHED FOR

*The Folger Shakespeare Library*

BY

CORNELL UNIVERSITY PRESS

*Ithaca, New York*

CORNELL UNIVERSITY PRESS

*First published 1963*

Library of Congress Catalog Card Number: 63-11494

PRINTED IN THE UNITED STATES OF AMERICA

BY VAIL-BALLOU PRESS, INC.

# Preface

PROFESSOR S. T. Bindoff deserves my gratitude for suggesting that I prepare this edition of Jewel's *Apology*. I wish to thank Louis B. Wright, Virginia LaMar, and Professor Roland M. Frye of the Folger Shakespeare Library for their interest and assistance. Jack Goodwin, librarian of the Virginia Theological Seminary, has provided his usual cheerful and valuable counsel and help. I must also acknowledge the continuing encouragement of Professor Horton Davies, Sir John Neale, and Robert Greaves. A person is indeed fortunate to live within the orbit of these careful and dedicated scholars.

J. E. B.

# Contents


Preface v

Introduction ix

Text 3

Part I 7

Part II 22

Part III 40

Part IV 51

Part V 83

Part VI 103

Recapitulation 134

The manner how the Church of England is administered and governed 139

Bibliography 147

Index 153

# Introduction

IN the spring of 1561 Queen Elizabeth I of England, together with her Councilors, made a decision, one of the consequences of which was the publishing of John Jewel's *Apology of the Church of England.* Although the religious settlement effected in the Parliament of 1559 was most definitely Protestant, there were those who tenaciously held on to the hope that Elizabeth would eventually rejoin the schismatic English Church to the See of Rome. Such hopes were ill founded, based upon such tenuous evidence as rumors at court and abroad and the deliberately misleading statements which the Queen made to over-anxious ambassadors. There were some actions too which kindled the hope. The retention of the cross or crucifix in the royal chapel is a well-documented illustration. While the royal visitation of 1559 was erasing the remnants of Romish superstition from the cathedrals and parish churches of England, Elizabeth insisted upon maintaining a cross or crucifix on the royal chapel altar, provoking John Jewel, then Bishop of Salisbury, to report to Peter Martyr, his Continental mentor:

Religion among us is in the same state which I have often described to you before. The doctrine is everywhere most pure; but as to ceremonies and maskings, there is a little too much foolery. That little silver cross, of ill-omened origin, still maintains its place in the

Queen's chapel. Wretched me! This thing will soon be drawn into a precedent.[1]

Thomas Sampson echoed Jewel's sentiments,[2] and Nicholas Throckmorton, English ambassador at Paris, believed that the royal practice was adversely affecting his nation's cause abroad. Thus he wrote to William Cecil, the Queen's principal secretary, concerning his efforts to make alliances with those of reformist tendencies in France: "I assure you, all that others which be of moment and all that I can do doth not so much further the cause as the cross and candlesticks in the Queen's Majesty's chapel doth hinder it."[3] But to the recusant John Martiall it was a cross of hope. In his *Treatyse of the Cross,* Martiall praised the Queen, "so well affectioned to the cross . . . that your Majesty have always kept it reverently in your chapel."[4] And Thomas Harding, writing from the center of English recusancy at Louvain, lauded Elizabeth for

your constant bearing and upholding of the banner and ensign of our redemption (the image I mean of Christ crucified), . . . your princely word commanding a preacher that opened his lewd mouth against the reverent use of the cross in your private chapel to retire from that ungodly digression unto his text.

The Queen's defense of the cross in her chapel signified to Harding that she had a "good inclination toward the ancient and catholic religion."[5]

The facts in the background, the Queen's education, training,

[1] *The Zurich Letters,* ed. Hastings Robinson, 1st ser. (Cambridge: Parker Society, 1842), p. 55.

[2] *Ibid.*, I, 63.

[3] P.R.O., S.P., 70/31, f. 86 recto, printed (in paraphrase) in *Calendar of State Papers, Foreign, 1562,* no. 618, p. 370.

[4] John Martiall, *A Treatyse of the Crosse* (Antwerp, 1564), sig. A. 2 verso.

[5] Thomas Harding, *A Confutation of a Booke intituled An Apologie of the Church of England* (Antwerp, 1565), sig. 2 verso.

environment, experience, and actions, were sometimes ignored or argued away. In the spring of 1561 there seemed to be at least a slim chance that Elizabeth would incline herself "toward the ancient and catholic religion" of the Roman See. Pope Pius IV wished to convey to her an invitation to send representatives to a new session of the Council of Trent. To some this seemed entirely feasible. To send royal representatives to the Council need not indicate any more than an inclination, need not indicate any final commitment to return to the Roman allegiance. With high hopes De Quadra, the King of Spain's envoy in London, urged the Queen and her Council to admit into the realm the papal nuncio, Martinengo, to hear the message and invitation which he brought from Rome.[6] In April the nuncio was in Brussels waiting for permission to cross the Channel.

Meanwhile, the question of admitting Martinengo was under debate in England. The Queen had kept informed, through her representative, concerning proceedings at Naumburg in February, when the German Protestant princes, having conferred with papal nuncios, rejected a similar invitation from the Pope.[7] This in itself would not have turned the tide, for Elizabeth had expressed her very great interest in a reunion of Christians and had seemed gratified at the approach of the nuncio. Such news De Quadra reported on April 14.[8] But by that time an event which was to influence the Queen's decision had already begun to happen. On April 14 a priest whose name was either Coxe or Devon was apprehended at Gravesend on his way from London to Flanders. On investigation a rosary and a breviary were discovered in his luggage. These evidences of recusancy caused the customs officials to send

[6] For details concerning Martinengo's mission, see C. G. Bayne, *Anglo-Roman Relations, 1558–1565* (Oxford Historical and Literary Studies, II; Oxford, 1913), chs. iv and v.

[7] Cf. P.R.O., S.P., 70/23, f. 29 recto.

[8] Bayne, p. 94.

the unfortunate man to the justice of the peace, before whom he accused Sir Thomas Wharton and Sir Edward Waldgrave of recusancy. Although it had not been the policy to enforce the statutes against recusancy rigidly or severely, Secretary Cecil seized upon the incident as providing a means for frustrating De Quadra's machinations and preventing the entrance of the nuncio. Therefore Coxe was dispatched to London, examined by Edmund Grindal, Bishop of London, and on April 17 order was taken to search the houses of Wharton and Waldgrave, together with the houses of others whom the priest had implicated. As a result a number of persons were imprisoned in the Tower amidst popular demonstrations against them. More arrests followed; several priests accused of casting spells to effect the Queen's death were seized; and the Marian bishops imprisoned at the Tower were kept under close guard, following a report that they hoped to be released as soon as the nuncio arrived. Rumors of conspiracy and treason were abroad and gave birth to more and more rumors, creating the impression that the admission of the nuncio was to signal the uprising of the papists in England against queen, parliament, and church.

At the end of April, De Quadra met with the Queen. It seems almost incredible that he still maintained hope. That he did is shown by a letter dispatched to the King of Spain, in which letter he explains that the Archbishops of Canterbury and York, the Bishops of Winchester and Salisbury (the latter being John Jewel), Nicholas Bacon, and William Cecil had been meeting to discuss the matter of the nuncio.[9]

On May 1 the decision was made. The Queen's Council, meeting at Greenwich, reported that the nuncio should be denied entrance into the kingdom for three reasons: First, to admit him would be to violate the laws, old and new, of the realm. Secondly, the coming of the nuncio would threaten the Queen's security. Thirdly, rebellion would be likely, as was in-

[9] *Calendar of State Papers, Spanish, 1558–1567,* p. 201.

dicated by those who lately had broken the laws of the realm and dispersed "abroad false and slanderous reports of the Queen's Majesty's disposition to change her religion and the government of this realm; a thing very false." [10] The news was communicated to De Quadra on May 5.[11] The following day the Spanish ambassador relayed the news to the Duchess of Parma, stating that the "harsh" report had been drawn up by the committee before mentioned: the Archbishops of Canterbury and York, the Bishops of Winchester and Salisbury, Nicholas Bacon, and William Cecil.[12]

Nothing further is known concerning this committee mentioned by De Quadra. It is possible that it was of his own creation, but there seems to be no evident reason why he should have invented it. Assuming that the committee did meet to discuss the nuncio's mission and the Pope's invitation in order to advise the Queen and her Council on the course of action to be followed, it is also quite possible that these same influential members of the government discussed the necessity of some public statement explaining the position of the English church and government in relation to the Council of Trent and the Papacy. Certainly once the decision had been made, it was necessary to explain the refusal to submit the English cause to arbitration at the Council of Trent.

It may be that Secretary Cecil was acting on matters discussed and decisions made by this little Greenwich committee, as well as by queen and council, when he wrote what is, for an understanding of the *Apology*, an especially important letter to the English ambassador in Paris. The Queen had already reported to Throckmorton her decision with regard to the nuncio. She assured him that she could never support a general council "where none shall have voice but the clergy that be sworn to the Pope." [13] On May 8 Cecil wrote to Paris reporting the same

[10] P.R.O., S.P., 12/17, f. 1 recto. [11] P.R.O., S.P., 12/26, no. 146.

[12] *CSP, Span., 1558–1567*, p. 204.

[13] P.R.O., S.P., 70/26, ff. 43 recto–44 verso, May 6, 1561.

news and replying to Throckmorton's report concerning false rumors spread abroad by papists.

I think you remember that since the last Lent you wrote of a slanderous report made there of our clergy and their variety. Surely I think that is no great cause to blame them, and saving three or four singular persons, as percase Mr. Album Caput,[14] etc., I know of no discrepancy amongst them, but for satisfaction of such doubt I have caused the Bishop of Sarum [Salisbury] to feign an epistle sent from hence thither, and have printed it secretly and send you herewith certain copies; if more be printed there, the matter shall have more probability. I have caused an apology to be written, but not printed, in the name of the whole clergy, which surely is wisely, learnedly, eloquently, and gravely written; but I stay the publishing of it until it may be further pondered, for so is it requisite.[15]

The first surviving notice of the *Apology* arises, then, in connection with the mission of the papal nuncio. It is no surprise, therefore, that the *Apology* deals at length with the authority of councils, the Council of Trent, and the rejection of papal primacy. However, the letter indicates that this was not the sole concern. The *Apology* is mentioned in conjunction with certain rumors circulated on the Continent concerning the English Church and its clergy. To what extent the Roman Catholic protagonists actually believed that the church in England was disastrously divided between contending and hostile groups cannot be ascertained. There were those who were convinced that among the consequences of such doctrines as justification by faith were immorality, division, and unrest, which would threaten the peace and security of any kingdom. The fragmentation of the common corps of Christendom resulting from the reformation movement was discerned by many. John Churchson, for one, Mary Tudor's chaplain, once wrote:

As now in our time, it is most open to every learned man what a contagious number of contrary sects hath issued, yea, burst out of

[14] I.e., Whitehead. [15] P.R.O., S.P., 70/26, f. 59 verso.

the puddle springs of Luther's heresies . . . whereof every one disagreeth from another and from verity itself, consenting against consent, agreeing almost in nothing but against agreement, divided in all things but in persecuting the unity of Christ his unical church . . .[16]

This unity of the church was assured in the medieval West by the primacy of the Roman bishop over all divisions of the church. Therefore in his life and teachings Martin Luther not only was accused of teaching heresy, which was serious enough, but of creating schism, the breach of love which utterly destroyed the spiritual welfare of the schismatic. It was to the issue of papal supremacy that the religious controversies of the sixteenth century continually returned. That the arguments over the Pope were inclined toward violence and invective, and are therefore offensive to modern students, is attributable to the fact that the combatants were fighting for their spiritual lives at a time when this was of ultimate concern. Thomas Dorman, in his controversy with Alexander Nowell, stated that he would concentrate his argument on a defense of the Papacy as the lawful head of the church.[17] Nowell agreed with the wisdom of this strategy: "May you once establish the Pope's authority, not to be denied, . . . you have won all, you need no Scriptures, no interpretation of doctors, no assembly of councils: all is in the box of the Pope's bosom."[18] Thomas Harding could not but be incensed with Nowell's way of stating it, but essentially he was in agreement concerning the centrality of papal au-

[16] John Churchson, *A brefe treatyse declaryng what and where the Churche is, that it is Knowen, and whereby it is tryed and Knowen* (London, 1556), sig. H. vii.

[17] Thomas Dorman, *A proufe of certeyne articles in religion denied by M. Iuell, sett furth in defence of the Catholyke beleef therein* (Antwerp, 1564), p. 3.

[18] Alexander Nowell, *A Reproufe . . . of a booke entituled, A Proufe of Certayne Articles in Religion denied by M. Iuell, set furth by Thomas Dorman* (London, 1565), p. 25.

thority. Thus he wrote: "As God commanded Moses and Aaron to be obeyed of the children of Israel, so Christ commanded all his sheep to obey and hear the voice of him whom in Peter, and succeeding Peter, he made shepherd over his whole flock." [19] According to Harding, the Protestants had founded a new church "set up by Satan through the ministry of Martin Luther and those other apostates his companions." [20]

Once the unity of the church had been broken through a rejection of papal supremacy, the processes of division took their own course. The Roman Catholic apologists saw the unending multiplication of sects contending with each other as well as with Rome and civil authority. The great danger in this to any kingdom was apparent, as Jerome Osorio pointed out to Queen Elizabeth, warning her that Protestants "go about to pull asunder the fences and inclosures of all law and religion." [21]

Immorality was believed to be a consequence of all this lawlessness and irreligion, of the teaching of the doctrine of justification by faith alone and the repudiation of papal authority. Robert Horne, later Bishop of Winchester, wrote in 1553 that he had heard reformers and their fellows called "drunkards, thieves, murderers, whoremongers, common brawlers." [22] In the Protestant attack upon the absolute necessity and legality of clerical celibacy, immoral and base motives were descried by the papists. Lewis Evans, a Roman Catholic who later turned Protestant, protested:

> What poor priest soever doth at this time live within the lurch of your [Protestant] injunctions and tyranny, the same is not accounted honest, zealous, nor earnest in faith unless he be clogged with a

[19] John Jewel, *A Defence of the Apologie of the Churche of Englande* (London, 1567), p. 17.

[20] Harding, *Confutation,* f. 42 recto.

[21] Jerome Osorio, *An Epistle . . . to the most excellent Princesse Elizabeth,* trans. Richard Shacklock (Antwerp, 1565), f. 27 recto.

[22] John Calvin, *Certain homilies . . . with an Apologie of Robert Horne* ([Rome?], 1553), preface, sig. A. viii verso.

quean, to carry him all headlong into hell. So that poor man which lived for a long time in chastity and perfection is now compelled to compass the love of some like damsel, to lead with her a loitering, detestable life, and so to bid farewell unto all his former faith, promise, and fidelity.[23]

Schismatic, heretical, divisive, immoral, such were the reformers and their ilk in England and everywhere. Against such accusations the English, government and clergy, reacted with intense feeling. The arguments of the accusers had to be refuted. And this they attempted with the counterargument that it was their papist enemies who were schismatic, heretical, divisive, and immoral.

To launch a counterattack as well as to record the truth concerning the English situation, Secretary Cecil set in motion a literary campaign.[24] He did this at the very time when clearer pronouncements were being made, more definite actions taken, revealing the religious and national position of England, revelations which would only increase the attacks emanating from Continental Roman Catholicism. A defense was in order, and a defense was launched with a certain "feigned" epistle and an apology.

Before examination of the writings themselves it is necessary to consider the man who was chosen to lead the literary offensive, the author of the *Apology,* John Jewel.[25] Jewel was born in 1522 at Buden near Ilfracombe in Devonshire. Little is

[23] Lewis Evans, *A brieve Admonition unto the nowe made Ministers of Englande: Wherein is shewed some of the fruicte of this theyr late framed fayth* (Antwerp, 1565), sigs. A. vi verso–A. vii recto.

[24] Cf. Conyers Read, *Mr. Secretary Cecil and Queen Elizabeth* (London, 1955), p. 262; Conyers Read, "William Cecil and Elizabethan Public Relations," in *Elizabethan Government and Society,* ed. S. T. Bindoff, Joel Hurstfield, and C. H. Williams (London, 1961), pp. 25–26.

[25] The first and still most important life of Jewel is Laurence Humphrey's *Ioannis Iuelli Angli, Episcopi Sarisburiensis vita & mors* (London, 1573). For a later biography based on Humphrey's, see C. W. Le Bas, *The Life of Bishop Jewel* (London, 1835).

known of his family, but it was far from affluent. After attending grammar schools in Devonshire, Jewel was sent by an uncle to Oxford. There he studied under John Parkhurst at Merton College. Parkhurst, with whom Jewel formed a lifelong friendship, was himself a Protestant and a humanist whose influence upon his student was considerable.[26] Having moved to Corpus Christi College, Jewel proceeded M.A. in 1545 and was then engaged as a Reader in Humanity and Rhetoric. In this teaching his humanist interests were exploited to the full. His students were set to work on Ovid and other Latin poets, Livy, and Cicero.[27] For Jewel, as for Parkhurst, humanism was the natural ally of the reformed faith, for they saw humanist studies breaking through the arid or corrupt accumulations of the recent past, providing the earnest student and convinced Christian the opportunity and the means for probing into the period of the primitive church and for recovering the Scriptures themselves from their medieval interpreters.

With the accession of Edward VI in 1547, evidence of Jewel's religious convictions increased. During this year Jewel received financial assistance for his studies on condition that he sign certain articles of faith. These articles involved rejection of the Papacy and of the scholastic doctrine of transubstantiation in the Mass as crass and impious.[28] At this time also, Peter Martyr Vermigli, the Italian reformer, heeded Cranmer's invitation and arrived at Oxford to become Regius Professor of Divinity there. Jewel was at once attracted to Martyr and became his ardent pupil and privileged friend until the Italian's death in 1562.

In 1551 Jewel was ordained and the next year took the B.D. degree. The sermon which he preached on this latter occasion indicated the extent of his reformed convictions. In it Jewel rejoiced that the light of the Gospel had broken out anew in his day. "There is none of us that ever was so blind," he said,

[26] Humphrey, p. 19. [27] *Ibid.*, pp. 27–28. [28] *Ibid.*, p. 32.

"that he saw not, or so blockish that he understood not, the calamity of former times." The superstition of the medieval church far surpassed that of the Jews, Egyptians, and Greeks. Transubstantiation, purgatory, celibacy, worship of saints, and images foisted upon the people were declared to be "new things . . . which the Scriptures never heard of. Whatsoever they cry and crake, they bring not a jot out of the word of God." The word of God, which the reformers recovered, had been displaced by "trifles, follies, baubles."

> These they honor instead of the word of God; upon these men suppose their salvation and the sum of religion to be grounded. And the which is more grievous, notwithstanding at this present, by the great goodness of God, religion is restored almost to her former dignity and light, yet poor and pitiful souls they set great store by these things.[29]

These "poor and pitiful souls" who honored men's creations more than God's word came into power in England with the accession of Mary Tudor. Jewel, then university orator, wrote a congratulatory letter to the Queen, although his heart must have been heavy. He could hope at least, as did others, that Mary would be lenient and move slowly. Peter Martyr returned to his home in Strasbourg and Jewel was deprived of his fellowship at Corpus. Rather than flee from England with his teacher and friend, Jewel chose to stay on at Oxford teaching a handful of loyal students and awaiting clearer indications of the trend of events. In April, 1554, he attended the trials of Cranmer and Ridley, acting as notary for the reformers. There the trend of events must have been obvious; his own freedom and safety were in jeopardy from that moment on.

It was then that Jewel committed an act which was for many

[29] John Jewel, *A Sermon made in Latine in Oxenforde, in the raigne of King Edward the sixt* (London, [1586?]), sig. C. For the Latin, see Humphrey, pp. 49 ff.

of his contemporaries, as well as for many writing in subsequent years, a blot on his character. Thomas Harding, writing against Jewel in the literary controversy, tells the story. Having been accused of inconstancy by Jewel for his turning from Protestantism to Roman Catholicism on the accession of Mary Tudor, Harding turned on Jewel and said:

> Are you not one M. John Jewel that in St. Mary's Church at Oxford subscribed openly, before the whole University, to the articles by the Catholics maintained, by the Gospelers impugned, after the Disputations there kept by learned men of both Universities against Cranmer, Ridley, and Latimer, whereat you were present, and did the office of notary, to report in writing all that was there done and said, and, after that you had heard the uttermost what could be said of your side, subscribed you not? [30]

Harding reported that the articles to which Jewel subscribed were two in number:

> That Christ's true and natural body and blood are verily and really present in the Sacrament of the altar under the forms of bread and wine.
>
> That the Mass is a sacrifice propitiatory for the quick and dead.[31]

When similarly accused by Henry Cole, Jewel made a reply that summed up his feelings on the matter: "I confess I should have done otherwise; but if I had not done as I did, I had not been here now to encounter with you." [32] Jewel thus defended his supposed betrayal and believed that actions subsequent to his signing the articles to a certain extent erased the shame. And yet inconstancy was viewed as a grievous evil at the time. Writers returned to the theme of inconstancy over and over

[30] Thomas Harding, *A Reioindre to M. Iewels Replie* (Antwerp, 1566), sig. CCCC. i.

[31] *Ibid.*

[32] John Jewel, *The true copies of the Letters betwene the reverend father in God Iohn Bisshop of Sarum and D. Cole* (London, 1560), sig. L. vii verso.

again. Indeed, in a time of constant change, revolutionary change, the word seemed most apt and descriptive. The anonymous translator of a little tract by Zwingli bemoaned many changes in the church between Henry VIII and Edward VI, changes which confused and confounded the laity. Referring to "diversity of preaching" and "new articles of their faith, made of new bishops in their new books of new institutions," he went on to bemoan this

> new inconstancy and inconstant novelty, now making, tomorrow marring; this year enacting, the next unacting; this day to be kept workday, the next year the same to be kept holy and idle; and suchlike of rooks, hares, and partridges. The simple people, I say, seeing this inconstancy, no marvel though they cannot tell whom nor what they may believe.[33]

Michal Wood accused Stephen Gardiner of inconstancy and asked his reader to mark "how Winchester runneth as it were a rash bedlam-brained hound, . . . rushing he careth not which way." [34] Augustine Bernher, Bishop Latimer's friend and servant, looked upon inconstancy as evil. He was not speaking of clergymen, but his description of inconstant gentlemen who change religion for the good of their businesses could with little effort become a description of priests who change religion to preserve their benefices. Bernher confronts the vacillating laity with the knowledge that the spirit of the Lord has departed from them.

> And this is more evident in your manifold and manifest perjuries, committed by you in King Henry's time, in King Edward's time, in Queen Mary's time. And what may be said of you at this time but

[33] Huldreich Zwingli, *The Rekening and declaration of the faith and beleif of Huldrik Zwingly bischoppe of Zuryk* (Zurich, 1543), A.iii.

[34] Stephen Gardiner, *De Vera Obediencia, An Oration made in Latine . . . And nowe translated into english and Printed bi Michal Wood* (Rouen, 1553), sig. A. iiij verso.

that you be false perjured hypocrites, bearing two faces under one hood, being ready like weathercocks to turn at all seasons as the wind doth carry you.[35]

The incident of Jewel's subscription to papist articles of faith was used by his enemies to discredit all his work on behalf of the English Church, with the implication that he was an unstable, vacillating, inconstant man. The strength of the argument lay in the common belief that martyrdom was preferable to inconstancy. Its weakness lay in the fact that many, including Thomas Harding, had changed their allegiance; Jewel was not alone in his instability, as he sought to prove when accused.

If by signing the articles Jewel had hoped to be left alone to live obscurely, as did Matthew Parker, he was deceived. Marshall, Dean of Christ Church, was intent upon seizing Jewel in order to send him on to Bonner, Bishop of London, for investigation and trial. Jewel heard of the plan and fled the country, arriving in Frankfort on March 13, 1555. There Jewel was welcomed by some men, but others had received reports of what he had done at Oxford and accused him of being "a stranger craftily brought in to preach, who had both been at Mass and also subscribed blasphemous Articles." [36] Jewel, with the advice of friends, confessed his error and asked for forgiveness. He then became involved in the struggle between two factions at Frankfort concerning the order of worship to be used among the exiles there. There were the followers of Richard Cox, later Bishop of Ely, who desired a modified form of the second *Book of Common Prayer* of Edward VI, and the followers of the Scottish reformer, John Knox, who wanted an order of worship patterned after that used in Geneva. In the struggle between the

[35] Hugh Latimer, *Certayn Godly Sermons . . . collected by Augustine Bernher* (London, 1562), epistle of Augustine Bernher to the Duchess of Suffolk, no pagination.

[36] *A Brief Discourse of the Troubles Begun at Frankfort,* ed. John Petheram (London, 1846), p. xlviii.

so-called Coxians and Knoxians, in which the former emerged victorious, Jewel was aligned with the more conservative Coxian party, the party whose national sentiment was most pronounced. Subsequently Jewel left Frankfort to join Peter Martyr in Strasbourg, and then followed his friend to Zurich when Martyr was called there. During this time Jewel continued his careful study of the writings of the early church fathers and observed and learned from the practices of the Swiss reformed churches. He established friendships then which he retained for the rest of his life, carrying on a vigorous correspondence with Martyr, Bullinger, and others.[37]

By December, 1558, the news of Mary's death and Elizabeth's accession had reached Zurich, and the Marian exiles hurried back to their home enthusiastic and hopeful. By March, 1559, Jewel was in London, where the Parliament was engaged in working out a new religious settlement. Jewel's first known involvement in Elizabethan affairs occurred in connection with the Westminster Disputation, ostensibly called to provide the members of the opposing religious parties an opportunity to arrive at some "good and charitable agreement." [38] Actually, as Sir John Neale says, it was intended to "serve as propaganda on which to launch the religious settlement." [39] Jewel himself believed that the disputation was being held so "that our bishops may have no ground of complaint that they are put down only by power and authority of law." [40] In the conference, Jewel was associated with the revolutionary reformers, who, with the ex-

[37] On Jewel and the Marian exiles, see M. M. Knappen, *Tudor Puritanism* (Chicago, 1939), pp. 118 f., 145; W. M. Southgate, "The Marian Exiles and the Influence of John Calvin," *History,* XXVII (1942), 148–152; reprinted in *The Making of English History,* ed. R. L. Schuyler and H. Ausubel (New York, [1952]).

[38] *The declaracyon of the procedynge of a conference, begon at Westminster the laste of Marche, 1559* (London, [1559?]).

[39] J. E. Neale, *Elizabeth I and Her Parliaments, 1559–1581* (London, 1953), p. 71.

[40] *Zurich Letters,* I, 10.

ception of Edmund Guest, later Bishop of Rochester, had been exiled during Mary's reign. They worked together to prepare arguments dealing with three articles or propositions which were obviously of their own choosing. Jewel summarizes these as follows:

> Our first proposition is that it is contrary to the word of God and the practice of the primitive church to use in the public prayers and administration of the sacraments any other language than what is understood by the people. The second is that every provincial church, even without the bidding of a general council, has power either to establish, or change, or abrogate ceremonies and ecclesiastical rites, wherever it may seem to make for edification. The third is that the propitiatory sacrifice, which the papists pretend to be in the Mass, cannot be proved by the Holy Scriptures.[41]

The disputation was, as might have been foreseen, more of a trial than a conference. Argument over procedural matters on the first day produced a situation resulting in the Roman Catholic defenders being held in contempt. The bishops rightly argued that this was not a disputation but a trial in which they were subjected to ill-treatment and abuse. However, it had the desired result, and the bishops, whose recalcitrance in the House of Lords had been amply demonstrated, casting negative votes against the Queen's program, were on their way out of office. Jewel benefited from this experience of working with fellow reformers under official auspices. Indeed, they were all of them, Jewel, Cox, Scory, Whitehead, Grindal, Horne, Sandys, Guest, Aylmer, destined for ecclesiastical preferment in the Elizabethan church. Their acceptance by the Queen and the government as necessary for the establishment and administration of the settlement of religion dates from the Westminster Disputation.

Subsequently Jewel was involved in the presentation of a declaration of faith by these same divines to the Queen. It is of interest to note that the declaration was inspired by the ac-

[41] *Ibid.*, p. 11.

cusations of their enemies. They wished to assure the Queen of their loyalty and orthodoxy. Thus they wrote that the papists accuse

> that our doctrine is detestable heresies, that we are fallen from the doctrine of Christ's catholic church, that we are subtle sectaries, that we dissent among ourselves, and that every man nourisheth and maintaineth his peculiar opinion, and that we be the teachers of carnal liberty, . . . that we be disordered persons, disturbers of the commonwealths, persuaders of rebellion, teachers of disobedience against our magistrates, and what not.[42]

Their concern was to refute the lies of their enemies by setting forth an orderly account of their faith, just as they had done "before the honorable auditory at Westminster." They desired to contest the rumors with a statement of their positive religious convictions. The Declaration of 1559, which Jewel with the others drew up for this purpose, standing between the Forty-two Articles of 1552 and the Thirty-nine of 1571, is a precursor of the *Apology,* as are also the documents prepared for use at the Westminster Disputation.

In the summer of 1559 Jewel was chosen for the bishopric of Salisbury, an honor he seemingly accepted with reluctance. As was the case with Matthew Parker, who was made Archbishop of Canterbury despite his protests, Jewel had lived the life of a college don and would have preferred an Oxford fellowship. His personal feelings counted for little, however, and when he set out for the western counties as a Royal Commissioner in the visitation of 1559 he carried the papers for his election with him. The visitation was designed to enforce the settlement of religion as described in the Statutes of Supremacy and Uniformity, as well as in the Articles and Injunctions of the visitation itself. Jewel then had ample opportunity to observe the condition of religion in England and to enforce a Protestant settlement on

[42] Corpus Christi College, Cambridge, MS 121, no. 20, pp. 139 f.

clergy and people. Returning to London on November 2, 1559, Jewel summed up his findings in a letter to Peter Martyr:

We found everywhere the people sufficiently well disposed toward religion, and even in those quarters where we expected most difficulty. It is however hardly credible what a harvest, or rather what a wilderness, of superstition had sprung up in the darkness of the Marian times. We found in all places votive relics of saints, nails with which the infatuated people dreamed that Christ had been pierced, and I know not what small fragments of the sacred cross.[43]

The cathedrals he found to be in desperate condition. Obstinacy was chiefly located among priests who had once been Protestant, men who "are now throwing all things into confusion." These had been displaced, but Jewel sensed a continuing danger. Much had been done; much remained to be accomplished. To Rudolph Gualter he wrote, on the same day:

The rage of the papists among us at this time is scarcely credible; and rather than seem to have been in error in any respect they most impotently precipitate and throw all things into confusion. May that God whose honor and glory alone we look to aid our endeavors and confound the conspiracies and wicked designs of his enemies.[44]

As a result of the visitation, Jewel was aroused to the danger remaining in the kingdom and was seemingly intent upon doing battle with the enemy. Thus on November 26 he went to Paul's Cross, the preaching station outside St. Paul's Cathedral, London, called by Thomas Carlyle "a kind of Times newspaper but edited partly by Heaven itself." [45] Before a great crowd Jewel issued a challenge to all papists, a challenge which was at the same time a defense.

If any learned man of all our adversaries, or if all the learned men that be alive, be able to bring any one sufficient sentence out of

[43] *Zurich Letters,* I, 44–45. [44] *Ibid.,* p. 48.

[45] Margaret E. Cornford, *Paul's Cross* (London, 1910), p. 75; Millar MacLure, *The Paul's Cross Sermons* (Toronto, 1958), p. 2.

> any old catholic doctor or father; or out of any old general council; or out of the Holy Scriptures of God; or any one example of the primitive church whereby it may be clearly and plainly proved that there was any private Mass in the whole world at that time, for the space of six hundred years after Christ, . . . [I will] give over and subscribe unto him.[46]

But it was not only private Mass which concerned Jewel. He presented the same challenge with regard to communion in one kind, prayers in a foreign tongue, the Pope as head of the church, Christ as substantially and carnally present in the Eucharist, transubstantiation, image worship, and many other of the practices and teaching of the papists which were abominable to the reformers. He was saying that these things, which England had renounced, were never taught or practiced in the early church and have no foundation in the Holy Scriptures. There is an echo here of the indictment made against "trifles, follies, baubles" many years before in the sermon which he preached when he received the B.D. degree.

The sermon aroused considerable interest. Jewel preached it at court and then at Paul's Cross once more in March, 1560. As he preached it again he expanded the items of the challenge until there were twenty-seven in all, mostly concerned with the Mass. He was clearly girding himself for battle and expressed his assurance that "they shall never be able truly to allege one sentence" in answer to the challenge.[47] That he perhaps was excessively confident was expressed not only by enemies but by such a friend as Alexander Nowell, Dean of St. Paul's,[48] but Jewel was certain that he was on the side of truth and that his enemies could never prevail against him. Such was the conviction of this man in a revolutionary age. In reality, Jewel was not proposing a scholarly disputation any more than

[46] John Jewel, *The copie of a Sermon pronounced by the Byshop of Salisburie at Paules Crosse* (London, 1560), sigs. F. vii recto–viii verso.

[47] *Ibid.*, sig. G. ii verso. [48] Nowell, sig. A. 2 verso.

the Westminster Disputation was intended to be such. He was waging warfare against an evil power which appeared to be the Antichrist foretold in the Apocalypse. Jewel and his fellows were convinced that they now lived in a church which was moving as near as could be to the primitive, pure church of the first six hundred years of Christian history, before Rome asserted its full primacy. The primitive church was an ideal for them because it had its foundation in the Scriptures and found its defense in the writings of the early church fathers and the decrees of the first four general councils. This association of Scriptures and primitive church was basic to the English establishment of religion and was honored in the statutes,[49] in the *Book of Common Prayer,* in the Ordinal, and by such eminent reformers as Thomas Cranmer and Nicholas Ridley.

Although it does not seem that Jewel seriously intended a scholarly disputation, almost at once the challenge was accepted and there began the long debate. The first contestant was Henry Cole, Marian Dean of St. Paul's Cathedral and a papist representative at the Westminster Disputation. Cole is a rather pitiable figure in the story. He was a prisoner in the Fleet, had not the freedom to prepare his counteroffense efficiently or well, and was misunderstood by Jewel. Jewel wanted Cole to defend every one of the items challenged, including the Pope as head of the church, whereas it appears that Cole was not a thoroughgoing papist but a conciliarist who believed with John Gerson that a general council of the church was superior to the Pope.[50] The results of their correspondence were published by Jewel to the advantage of the English Church and in defense of the Elizabethan establishment.[51]

During the rest of 1560 Jewel remained in his diocese conducting a visitation and doing other necessary business. He re-

[49] I Eliz., cap. 1, sec. 20.
[50] Cf. T. M. Veech, *Dr. Nicholas Sanders* (Louvain, 1935), p. 76.
[51] Jewel, *The true copies of the Letters.*

turned to London at the beginning of 1561, to become a key figure in the rising literary campaign against Rome. Sometime after his arrival and while the question of the nuncio was being discussed, Cecil set Jewel to work writing a treatise that would explain and defend the English reformation. The sequence of events, with the refusal of the nuncio and the pronouncement against the Council of Trent and the Papacy, probably called for various additions and expansions to be made. For instance, once the decision had been made with regard to Martinengo and Trent, a defense of that decision would be necessary. Therefore, it seems evident, the printing of the *Apology* was deferred. But there was some urgency with regard to the rumors which Throckmorton had reported, rumors accusing the English clergy of dissension and variety. In order to meet the immediate need and to allow for more time in which to alter the *Apology* to the satisfaction of Cecil, Jewel was asked by the Queen's secretary to write a letter, under an assumed name, a letter refuting the rumors.

This letter is entitled *Epistola cuiusdam Angli, qua asseritur consensus verae religionis doctrinae & caeraemoniarum in Anglia, contra vanissimos quorundam cavillos, quibus eandem suis ad plebeculam contionibus impugnare conantur*[52] ("The letter of a certain Englishman, in which is asserted the consensus of true religion, doctrine, and ceremonies in England, against the empty scoffing of some who try to impugn this truth in their sermons to the simple people"). It is said to be a letter from "Nicholas N., Englishman, to John N., an old friend living

[52] Identified as Jewel's "lost" epistle by the present writer, the only known copy of this printed work is to be found in the British Museum. It has the date 1561. The staff of the British Museum states that it was definitely not printed in England. No place of publication and no printer's device is provided. A manuscript copy is to be found in the P.R.O., S.P., Eliz., 12/16, no. 46. Cf. the present writer's forthcoming *John Jewel, Apologist of the Church of England* for an edition of the Latin together with an English translation.

in Paris." [53] It begins by stating that it is an answer to those who say that the English clergy

> are split into factions and sects by partialities and arguments; that among us nothing is certain; that there is agreement neither of bishops among themselves, nor preachers, nor ministers of the church, nor individual men, either about doctrine or about ceremonies; that everyone makes his own church for himself according to his whim.

After castigating the monks who spread the rumors and the French for believing them, Jewel went on to assert that which he was certain was the truth.

> We indeed are all in agreement among ourselves about every part of religion, about God, about Christ, about the justification of man, the Scriptures, the church, the sacraments, the magistrates, and about ecclesiastical polity.

Jewel then argued that perhaps the accusers would concede the unity of the English clergy with regard to doctrine, but would "make a case against us about ceremonies."

> It appears that all that talk and contention of parties comes back finally to this. Among a few people there is some difference in some vestments and skullcaps. That, as I might confess, has always been true to some extent, for in this matter our predecessors have always retained some liberty.

Jewel was quite aware that there were some who protested against the wearing of the vestments prescribed by the Ornaments Rubrics and the bishops. Jewel himself protested against wearing garb tainted by long use in the Church of Rome. But however undesirable it might be, the matter of variety in the use of vestments was a thing of indifference to him. "Everybody is enough convinced, even the prince who commanded these things, that clothing is nothing so far as religion is concerned,

[53] I am indebted to Mr. Paul Larkin and the Reverend Richard Reid for assistance with the English translation used here.

that there is in clothing neither any holiness nor any contagion." Therefore let there be some variety in unimportant affairs, as there has always been some freedom concerning such matters in the church, even from the beginning of the church.

There then follows a section strikingly reminiscent of the third part of the *Apology*, beginning:

Those who so tragically ridicule us, O immortal God, how beautifully do they agree among themselves? Or do these your little brothers and monks raise these objections against us, to whom there was scarcely anything common besides the light and air, who for so many years were never in agreement among themselves about vesture, or prayers, or tonsures, or bows, or tunics, or palls, or sandals, or form, or color, or food, or drink?

The accusers, the rumormongers, are the ones who disagree and wage bitter fights amongst themselves. The English, if they do disagree, do so in a friendly manner and "unanimously and with one mouth . . . glorify God and the Father of our Lord Jesus Christ." Jewel ended by recalling his readers to the Holy Scriptures. "As many times as you hear those monks of yours to be upset, each time consider a trap to be set for you by the devil, that you should lose your salvation and think badly of the Gospel of Christ."

The technique revealed in this letter is familiar to the student of the *Apology* and was used in previous controversial literature. There is a discussion of the necessity for the treatise, a recounting of the accusations made, and a discussion of their falsehood. There then follows a positive assertion setting the truth alongside the falsehood. Lastly there is a counterattack in which the accusations made against the English are turned against the enemy. Insofar as methodology is concerned, the *Epistola* represents a reasonably clear outline of the *Apology* itself.

There is no further information concerning this little pamphlet. Not even Throckmorton, to whom it was sent, speaks of it in his correspondence with Cecil following the date on which it was sent to him. Indeed, the ambassador continued to urge Cecil to commission the production of an apology. His reasons for making this request were varied and went beyond the necessity of refuting rumors concerning the variety of the English clergy. He was particularly interested to see printed a dissertation on English reformed doctrine which he could use in his dealing with French leaders, who were tending toward a reformed position but disliked Lutheranism and were fearful of Calvinism, then stirring up passions in France. With this in mind Throckmorton wrote to Cecil in May, 1561.[54] By August, Parker was expressing some distress that the *Apology* was not available for use at the conference of Poissy.[55] In December, Throckmorton was complaining that the writing needed was still not available. He stated once more the great need for some learned men to write an apology in Latin, using a certain modesty "to avoid as much as may be to irritate any party."[56] At that time the *Apology* must have been in the hands of the printer, although Throckmorton seemingly was not informed of the fact. And then, on January 24, 1562, the ambassador acknowledged seeing a copy of "the Bishop of Salisbury's apology."[57] Two days later he had received his copy of it from Cecil. In his letter of thanks he commended Parker and Jewel for the book, but expressed disappointment that while the papists were well answered in it, the Calvinists were not dealt with. Furthermore, he disliked the offensive language used in the *Apology*. "At this time humors be so stirred in all men that they be too prompt to be irritate with small things."[58]

The text that this volume presents is an English translation of

[54] Cf. P.R.O., S.P., 70/26, no. 180, f. 135.

[55] Matthew Parker, *Correspondence, 1535–1575*, ed. J. Bruce and T. T. Perowne (Cambridge: Parker Society, 1853), p. 148.

[56] P.R.O., S.P., 70/33, f. 103.

[57] P.R.O., S.P., 70/34, f. 36 verso–37 recto.

[58] P.R.O., S.P., 70/34, f. 114 recto.

the *Apologia Ecclesiae Anglicanae* which Throckmorton read. The first part of the work begins with the statement that "truth wandereth here and there as a stranger in the world and doth readily find enemies and slanderers amongst those that know her not." The patriarchs and prophets of the Old Testament were misunderstood and assailed. Christ himself was called Beelzebub, "a deceiver of the people, a drunkard, and a glutton." Knowing that these, together with the apostles and early Christians, were thus treated, "we ought to bear it more quietly . . . if we for the same cause be handled after like sort." Jewel then considered what was said against the sixteenth-century Christians of the reformed faith, how they were called heretics, disturbers of godly order, sowers of sects, men who disagree and are at variance with each other. It is necessary, then, that the English clergy defend themselves, "our own cause and innocency," following the examples of Christ, St. Paul, and the early Christian apologists. Especially is this requisite seeing that Pope Paul IV condemned so large a part of the world without hearing any defense of its actions.

Because the Pope has prevented the English from a free voice in the Council of Trent, except they yield to his supremacy, "for this cause chiefly we thought it good to yield up an account of our faith in writing." The *Apology* is meant, therefore, to explain the position of the English in relation to the Council and to the world; it is in a sense conceived to be a means by which to have a free voice. The truth will be shown that the Scriptures and early church fathers support the English who have left the Roman Church with just cause and have "returned to the apostles and old catholic fathers."

Jewel ended his introduction by calling upon the enemy to prove their cause by the Scriptures. The Scriptures have ever been the basis upon which doctrine and practice have been tried and heresy detected. But he knows that they will not agree to this, for they have preferred, instead of the Scriptures, "their own dreams and full cold inventions; and, to maintain their own traditions, have defaced and corrupted, now these many hundred years, the ordinances of Christ and his apostles."

For two reasons, then, the *Apology* is presented: to present the truth and thus refute the rumors and lies spread against the English clergy, and to demonstrate the manifold errors of the papists that prevent the English from joining in the Council of Trent.

The second part of the work then proceeds with a summary of the doctrinal beliefs of the English clergy, those things upon which they are agreed. Each paragraph begins with "We believe," and the whole follows the usual form of a creed, with statements regarding the Trinity, Christ, the Holy Ghost, and the church. Then other matters are brought in and dealt with at greater length: the threefold ministry of bishops, priests, and deacons, their power and authority over the laity, and their right to marry; the canon of Scripture and its authority; the two dominical sacraments of baptism and Eucharist, with a lengthy and important discussion of the latter; purgatory; ceremonies; prayer in the vulgar tongue; Christ as the only mediator between man and God; the reformation doctrine of justification by faith alone; and the resurrection of the flesh. Here then is the faith of the English Church.

In Part III Jewel attacked the accusation that the English "have fallen into sundry sects" and disagree amongst themselves. First he denies that the preachers of the Gospel have any responsibility for the rise of heresy in numerous sects, and then he asserts his conviction that Rome is to be held responsible for this plague. That there is some division of opinion in England in religious matters he does not deny, but refers to the Scriptures and the early church, where such division existed without extinguishing the light of the Gospel. The English are accused of being divided between Lutherans and Zwinglians, but Jewel ridicules this, for their unity greatly outweighs the disagreement over the one trifling doctrine of the mode of Christ's presence in the Eucharist. He then turns the attack back upon the Roman Catholics, pointing to their many serious divisions during the Middle Ages and the sixteenth century. From the question of unity, which Jewel will not elevate above the question of truth, truth being of far greater importance than unity, the argument shifts to the accusation that the Reformation has bred immorality. He does not seek to present the Protestants as morally pure, but he asserts that evil in the midst of purity is easily found out.

In the fourth part Jewel sought to expose the immorality rampant amongst the papists: canon lawyers advocating fornication; bawds and concubines openly seen in Rome; adultery, murder, incest unpunished in the church. The accusation that the Protestants stir up rebellions and civil disobedience then received attention. Protesting that the charge is false, Jewel attempted to turn this accusation back against the enemy. Next the assertion that the English have broken the unity of the church and have departed from the true church is confronted. Here Jewel is concerned to show that Rome is not the true church by the common standards of judgment, by the examples of the Scriptures and the primitive church, "which we doubt not but was indeed the true catholic church." Here there follows an attack upon "the tyranny of the Bishops of Rome, and their barbarous Persian-like pride" and the papists' lack of regard for the Holy Scriptures. The Scriptures they call "a bare letter, uncertain, unprofitable, dumb, killing, and dead . . . like to a nose of wax" which can be turned this way and that. Above the Scriptures they place the church, and the Pope above the church. This, Jewel asserts, is evil, for the Scriptures are God's own word. The papists have not the Scriptures, but they contend that they have the primitive church to support them.

Part V begins with an attempt to demonstrate that the papists do not have the ancient church on their side, that they have departed from the example of that church. In considerable detail Jewel cites fathers and councils which commanded those very things which the papists refuse, the Roman Catholics putting in the place of necessary things mere "chaff instead of wheat," deceiving and ruining the people. Considering how evil this Roman Church is which claims it cannot err, it is only right that men should depart from her.

We truly have renounced that church wherein we could neither have the word of God sincerely taught, nor the sacraments rightly administered, nor the name of God duly called upon. . . . And we are come to that church wherein they themselves cannot deny (if they will say truly, and as they think in their own conscience) but all things be governed purely and reverently, and, as much as we possibly could, very near to the order used in the old time.

The question of the general council provided the beginning for the sixth part of the *Apology*. The papists will say that the English had no right to act as they did without the consent of a general council of the church. Jewel states that the religious settlement was dealt with in parliament and convocation as was right and necessary; that the Council of Trent is subservient to the Pope and not fit to decide the affairs of Christians. Jewel then turns to consider the authority of the Christian princes, princes excluded by the Papacy from governing the church. Using the examples of the Old Testament and the primitive church, Jewel asserts the right of princes to govern the religious establishments in their own realms. The first four general councils of the church were called together by civil magistrates who took part in their discussions. Here Jewel is defending the royal supremacy, although he does not speak explicitly and in detail of it in the *Apology*. Nevertheless, the English Reformation has been achieved under a Christian prince and with Christians assembled in parliament and convocation. It was rightly accomplished, recalling the erring church, the church which was itself heretical and schismatic, to the "church of the apostles and of the old catholic bishops and fathers." The matter could not await the calling of a general council of Christendom; and besides, "the truth of the Gospel of Jesus Christ dependeth not upon councils, nor, as St. Paul saith, upon mortal creatures' judgments. . . . God is able (not only without councils, but also, will the councils, nill the councils) to maintain and advance his own kingdom." With a final attack upon the Pope, this last part of the *Apology* comes to an end with a summary or recapitulation of the argument. Here the dual chords are struck again: the assertion of unity against accusations of disunity; the defense of England's refusal to submit its cause to the Council of Trent and the Papacy. Then too, the refrain, which becomes familiar as the *Apology* is read through and as the literature of the English church is perused, is sounded once more:

We have searched out of the Holy Bible, which we are sure cannot deceive, one sure form of religion, and have returned again unto the primitive church of the ancient fathers and apostles, that is to say, to the first ground and beginning of things, as unto the very foundations and headsprings of Christ's church.

If Throckmorton was disturbed by the violence of the final product, others had only effusive praise for the *Apology*. Peter Martyr wrote from Zurich that the book

hath not only in all points and respects satisfied me, . . . but it appeared also to Bullinger, and his sons and sons-in-law, and also to Gualter and Wolfius, so wise, admirable, and eloquent, that they can make no end of commending it, and that nothing in these days hath been set forth more perfectly.[59]

There seemed no doubt in Martyr's mind that Jewel was the sole author of the Latin work, which bore no indication of authorship. During the subsequent years there was some questioning of the matter, although Jewel as the chief person responsible for the work has always been recognized as its author.

[59] *Zurich Letters,* I, 339.

The problem arises because men often referred to the book by name without mentioning Jewel, as was true of Cecil himself when writing to Parker about it.[60] But then too, the work was intended to represent the views of all the English clergy and not just one man; therefore it was not intended at the outset that it should be too closely identified with Jewel himself. Secondly, Cecil and Parker obviously were connected with the production of the book, Cecil having commissioned it and Parker acting as editor. Lastly, in such an enterprise as this it would be understandable if Jewel obtained assistance from others of the divines with whom he had worked in the Westminster Disputation and in the preparation of the Declaration of Faith, not to mention the little Greenwich committee. Parker, as a preface to the 1564 translation, wrote a letter to Lady Bacon in which he made a statement understandable in the light of the above considerations: "And whereas both the chief author of the Latin work and I, severally perusing and conferring your whole translation. . . ."[61] Jewel was the chief author, his name is therefore rightly attached to the work, but he did not bear the responsibility for it entirely alone.

The *Apology* was widely distributed. Besides the Latin original and two English translations to be discussed later, Jewel reported that it was

> imprinted in Latin at Paris and hath been sithence translated into the French, the Italian, the Dutch, and the Spanish tongues, and hath been sent and borne abroad into France, Flanders, Germany, Spain, Pool [Poland], Hungary, Denmark, Sveveland [Sweden], Scotland, Italy, Naples, and Rome itself to the judgment and trial of the whole Church of God. Yea, it was read and sharply considered in your late Covent at Trent, and great threats made there that it should be answered: and the matter by two notable learned bishops taken in hand, the one a Spaniard, the other an Italian.[62]

[60] Parker, pp. 161–162.
[61] See the letter preceding the text of the *Apology* on p. 3.
[62] Jewel, *Defence* (1567), p. 28.

Nothing is now known of an answer to the *Apology* by a Spaniard and an Italian, but shortly after Jewel's book appeared many set about to do battle with it. Indeed, the literary controversy that resulted after the appearance of the Challenge Sermon of 1559–1560 and the *Apology* came to involve so many disputants that it is now known as "the Great Controversy." [63] The English recusants living at Louvain were responsible for producing forty-one volumes against Jewel and his fellows, all between the years 1564 and 1568.[64]

The chief English scholar at Louvain was Nicholas Sanders, who was aided by Thomas Harding, Thomas Stapleton, John Martiall, Richard Shacklock, Thomas Heskyns, Robert Pointz, and William Allen. This team of men wrote chiefly in English for the distribution of their books in England. As Thomas Veech says:

> The efforts of the exiles at Louvain were directed to the practical end of providing a stimulus to the Catholics in England, weakened by the persecution combined with the unceasing struggle of the Anglican divines to win over the dispirited members of the party.[65]

The books, intended to refute the arguments of Jewel, were smuggled into England and distributed in spite of the action taken by the English government to halt the illegal practice.[66]

The first published work of the controversy was Jewel's collection of the correspondence between himself and Henry Cole. There then followed Thomas Harding's *An Answere to Maister Iuelles Chalenge,* printed in 1564 but circulated in manuscript two years earlier. An anonymous *Apologie of Private Masse* (1562) carried on the reply to Jewel's challenge and was an-

[63] Cf. A. C. Southern, *Elizabethan Recusant Prose, 1559–1582* (London, [1950]), for an account of the literature of the controversy.

[64] Cf. J. H. Pollen, *The English Catholics in the Reign of Queen Elizabeth* (London, 1920), p. 107.

[65] Veech, p. 99.

[66] Cf. Veech, p. 101; Southern, pp. 33 ff.; John Rastell, *A Treatise intitled, Beware of M. Iewel* (Antwerp, 1566), sig. B. j verso.

swered by Thomas Cooper, Bishop of Lincoln. Also in 1562 the venerable Richard Smith wrote his *Confutatio eorum quae Phil. Melancthon obijcit contra missae sacrificium propitiatorium,* which was published at Louvain against both Challenge Sermon and *Apology.* John Rastell and John Martiall wrote against the sermon, and the latter was answered by James Calfhill, one of the early Puritan divines. Thomas Dorman then entered the fray in 1564 with his *A proufe of certeyne articles of religion denied by M. Iuell,* attacking both sermon and *Apology.* Alexander Nowell, Dean of St. Paul's Cathedral, took on Dorman in an interesting exchange involving five books in four years.

But it was the president of Oxford House at Louvain, Thomas Harding, with whom Jewel chose to do combat. Perhaps this was because of the close ties which had bound them together earlier, ties severed by their settling in opposite camps. Like Jewel, Harding came from Devonshire, where he was born in 1516. The two men attended the same school in Barnstaple, although at different times. They met at Oxford, where Harding was a student and then fellow of New College. They were both won over to Protestant convictions and felt the influence of Peter Martyr; they both subscribed to Roman articles during Mary's reign, although Harding did not renounce his subscription as did Jewel. They met, for the last time, in 1559 at Salisbury, where Harding was a member of the Cathedral chapter and Jewel was a Royal Commissioner. Harding saw Jewel elected Bishop of Salisbury; Jewel saw Harding deprived of his livings. When Harding then wrote against Jewel, there was personal antagonism between the two men, antagonism which occasionally broke into the theological arguments and helps to account for some of the vehemency of the writings of the two men.[67]

[67] Cf. John Jewel, *A Replie unto M. Hardinges Answeare* (London, 1566), sig. IIi. 2 verso; Harding, *Reioindre* (1566), sig. CCC. i ff.

Harding's *Answer* of 1564 brought forth Jewel's *A Replie unto M. Hardinges Answeare* (1565). Harding then wrote *A Reioindre to M. Iewel's Replie* (1566), against the first article of the Challenge, to which Edward Dering answered, and subsequently *A Reioindre to M. Iewel's Replie against the Sacrifice of the Masse* (1567). This ended the dispute over the Challenge. As the controversy concerning the twenty-seven points under debate developed, the writings became more and more detailed, more lengthy, more repetitious, until Harding was writing one book for just one of the articles.

Their debate over the *Apology* began with Harding's *A Confutation of a Booke intituled An Apologie of the Church of England,* published in 1565. Jewel answered with his massive *Defence of the Apologie of the Churche of Englande* (1567), in which he attempted to respond to each of Harding's criticisms. Harding then selected what seemed to him to be the most important and vulnerable sections of the *Defence,* concerning which he wrote *A Detection of sundrie foule errours, lies, sclaunders, corruptions, and other matters, uttered and practized by M. Iewel, in a Booke lately by him set foorth entituled, A Defence of the Apologie &c.* (1568). Jewel then brought out an enlarged edition of the *Defence* which undertook to answer Harding's *Detection,* this in June of 1570, less than a year before his death.

In all of these writings the contenders were attempting to show support for their separate causes from the Scriptures and from the fathers and councils of the primitive church. At the same time they sought to discredit their opponents by demonstrating that they were liars and falsifiers of Scripture and the primitive church. The readers whom they sought to influence were constantly remembered. Both sides, convinced that they possessed the truth to the exclusion of all others, sought every means to discredit the opposition and thereby to retain or win adherents. Thus there are many, many lengthy quotations from fathers,

Scriptures, councils, decretals, the pagan classics, and from works by contemporary theologians and historians. Thus also a great effort was made to expose every minor, trivial error, in the belief that the accumulation of many small mistakes convicts the opposition of gross mishandling of the evidence. Contrary to the general reaction in our own day, the diatribe and abuse, the catalogues of quotations and references, were not considered out of place in the sixteenth century. In England, Jewel's work was highly praised, and the *Apology* itself was held in high esteem as an authoritative indictment of Rome and defense of England.

Parker, as Archbishop of Canterbury and editor of the *Apology*, had planned to have convocation in 1563 join articles of religion to a revised *Apology*, the two in one book "by common assent to be authorized, as containing true doctrine, and enjoined to be taught to the youth in the universities and grammar schools throughout the realm." [68] The Earl of Warwick in 1568 advised Parker to order that "every minister may be bound to have" a copy of the *Defence*.[69] Parker urged Parkhurst, Bishop of Norwich, in 1573, to see to it that the *Defence* was "had in the rest of the parish churches within your diocese." [70] Articles and injunctions [71] and churchwardens' account books [72] provide evidence of the official nature of the book placed in parish churches for the edification of clergy and people. And then in 1609 Archbishop Bancroft saw a wish fulfilled when the works of Jewel were printed in one volume in order that every parish church should have a copy.[73] As late as 1938, Jewel's *Defence of the Apology* or his *Works* (1609 or 1611) were to be found chained

[68] John Strype, *Annals of the Reformation* (Oxford, 1820–1840), I, i, 474.

[69] Parker, p. 319. [70] *Ibid.*, pp. 416–417.

[71] Cf. W. P. M. Kennedy, *Elizabethan Episcopal Administration* (London, 1924), II, 79, Barnes's injunctions of 1577.

[72] *Historical Manuscripts Commission, 5th Report,* p. 573; "Elizabethan Churchwardens' Accounts," ed. J. E. M. Farmiloe and R. Nixseaman, *Bedfordshire Historical Record Society,* XXXIII (1953), 11.

[73] E. Cardwell, *Documentary Annals of the Reformed Church of England* (Oxford, 1844), II, 126.

in thirteen different cathedrals and parish churches in England.[74]

Mandell Creighton, writing in the last century, called the *Apology* and its *Defence* "the first methodical statement of the position of the Church of England against the Church of Rome, and . . . the groundwork of all subsequent controversy." [75] That the author and the work were most highly esteemed by those who lived after Jewel is evident. In the literature of the vestiarian controversy of 1566 Jewel's works were claimed in support of both Puritans and defenders of the establishment.[76] In the admonitions controversy commencing in 1571, both Cartwright and Whitgift acknowledged Jewel's greatness, Whitgift stating that it was not necessary to recite the articles of faith held by the Church of England "for they be at large set out in sundry English books, and especially in the Apology of the Church of England and the Defence of the same." [77] Richard Hooker, author of *The Laws of Ecclesiastical Polity,* enjoyed Jewel's patronage when a student at Oxford, read Jewel's works there,[78] and later wrote that he considered the Bishop of Salisbury to be "the worthiest divine that Christendom hath bred for some hundreds of years." [79] And Lancelot Andrewes, one of the greatest of the Caroline divines, wrote in his *Concio Latine habita:* "En Ecclesiae nostrae Apologiam vere Gemmeam." [80]

The importance of the *Apology* cannot be denied. It grew out of the events of the times, was commissioned by the govern-

[74] H. J. Cowell, *The Four Chained Books* (London, 1938), 35.

[75] *DNB*, under Jewel.

[76] Cf. *A briefe discourse against the outwarde apparell and ministring garmentes of the popishe church* ([n.p.], 1566), sig. C. iiij verso; *A briefe examination . . . of a certaine declaration lately put in print in the name and defence of certaine ministers in London refusyng to weare the apparell prescribed by the lawes and orders of the Realme* (London, [1566?]), sigs. ****** 2 verso–****** 3 recto.

[77] John Whitgift, *Works,* ed. J. Ayre (Cambridge: Parker Society, 1852), I, 3.

[78] Cf. *Notes and Queries,* 2nd ser., XI (London, 1861), 221–223.

[79] R. Hooker, *The Laws of Ecclesiastical Polity,* bk. II, sec. 6(4) (London, 1907), I, 260.

[80] Lancelot Andrewes, *Opuscula quaedam posthuma* (Oxford, 1852), p. 90.

ment as an explanation and defense of the position taken by the Elizabethan church against Rome. As such it is worthy of study. But it also encompasses, particularly in the second part, an explanation of the doctrinal beliefs of the English Church, and in other parts discusses the basis of the English reform movement and defends its acknowledgment of royal supremacy. Here, then, the teachings of the church are set forth to be studied in relation to the articles of religion, the homilies, the *Book of Common Prayer*, and other formularies by the student of history who wishes to understand the reformed theology as expounded in England.

Of great importance, also, is the evidence which the work provides of the ecumenical character of English theology in the first part of the Elizabethan period. While in the second part of the *Apology* the doctrine concerning the real presence in the Eucharist is neither Lutheran, espousing consubstantiation, nor Zwinglian, espousing "mere memorialism," yet the assertions made concerning sacraments in general and the Eucharist in particular do not differ significantly from the teachings of Peter Martyr Vermigli, Martin Bucer, or John Calvin.[81] The same can be said with regard to the doctrine of the church, the basis for doctrinal authority, and the teaching with regard to church and state relationships.[82] At the same time, it must be admitted that the *Apology* was written with a conscious endeavor to remain faithful to earlier English formularies. The second part of the work is related to the developing series of articles of

[81] For instance, see the statement: "We affirm that bread and wine are heavenly mysteries of the body and blood of Christ, and that by them Christ himself, being the true bread of eternal life, is so presently given unto us, as that by faith we verily receive his body and blood" (*Apology*, pt. II). Cf. Darwell Stone, *A History of the Doctrine of the Holy Eucharist* (London, 1909), II, 225; J. C. McLelland, *The Visible Words of God* (Edinburgh, 1957), p. 217; G. J. van de Poll, *Martin Bucer's Liturgical Ideas* (Assen, 1954), pp. 85 ff.

[82] Cf. W. M. Southgate, *John Jewel and the Problem of Doctrinal Authority* (Cambridge, Mass., 1962).

religion extending from those devised under Henry VIII to the Declaration of Religion of 1559 and the Eleven Articles of 1561. And yet too much emphasis must not be placed upon the distinctively English development. Cautious as it was, conciliatory as it needed to be, the English Reformation was being constantly influenced by the Continental Reformation, and the *Apology* itself was widely accepted by Continental reformers.[83] Indeed, Jewel seemed most anxious to retain doctrinal unity with the Swiss Reformation and rejoiced to say, when speaking of the Declaration of 1559, that "we have exhibited to the Queen all our articles of religion and doctrine, and have not departed in the slightest degree from the confession of Zurich." [84] It may not be too much to claim, then, that one who reads the *Apology* will make contact with the spirit of the Reformation in a general sense, realizing that Jewel, like Cranmer, believed that the bonds uniting the reformers were stronger and far more important than the issues which separated them.

The present edition of the *Apology* is the second English translation of the Latin work. Shortly after the appearance of the *Apologia Ecclesiae Anglicanae,* Archbishop Parker determined that a translation should be made for use in England.[85] The work was done, but the identity of the translator is unknown. Whoever it was, we can be sure that it was someone in a position of authority for, in the process of translating the Latin, corrections and additions were made.[86] The inadequacies and inaccuracies of this translation made it imperative that another translator be found. According to Parker's letter, this

[83] See letter of Peter Martyr previously cited (*Zurich Letters,* I, 339).

[84] *Zurich Letters,* I, 21.

[85] Cf. John Jewel, *Works,* ed. J. Ayre (Cambridge: Parker Society, 1850), IV, xviii; *A Transcript of the Registers of the Company of Stationers of London, 1554–1640,* ed. E. Arber (London and Birmingham, 1875–1894), I, 178.

[86] Cf. *An Apologie, or aunswer in defence of the Church of England, concerninge the state of Religion used in the same* (London, 1562), ff. 38 recto–39 recto.

new translation was provided, unsolicited, by Lady Ann Bacon. This eminent woman was one of the learned Cooke sisters, the daughter of Sir Anthony Cooke, tutor to Edward VI and Privy Councilor under Elizabeth I. Lady Bacon was born in 1528, schooled in a rigorous manner, and was reputedly learned in Latin, Greek, Italian, and French. She married Sir Nicholas Bacon in 1556 or 1557 and had as her sons Anthony, the diplomatist, and Francis, the Lord Chancellor, philosopher, and lawyer. A woman of strong Puritan sympathies, she translated into English from the Latin certain sermons of the reformer Bernardino Ochino. So revered was she by Calvin's successor in Geneva, Theodore Beza, that he dedicated his *Meditations* to her.[87]

It was this woman who translated that which became the official English version of the *Apology*, the version used with but minor changes by Jewel himself in his controversy with Harding. Parker paid her translation high praise in the sixteenth century, and in the twentieth C. S. Lewis has said that "if quality without bulk were enough, Lady Bacon might be put forward as the best of all sixteenth-century translators."[88]

Appended to the Bacon translation of 1564 were two short pieces reproduced in the present edition. The first is the letter of Parker to the translator, already mentioned. At the end there is a longer tract for which Parker himself was most likely responsible. This is entitled: "The manner how the Church of England is administered and governed."

The purpose of this edition is to make the *Apology* available to as wide a reading public as possible. I have, therefore, based the text upon the 1564 edition, the Bacon translation. In a few

[87] On Lady Bacon cf. *DNB,* under Ann Bacon; M. St. C. Byrne, "The Mother of Francis Bacon," *Blackwood's Magazine,* CCXXXVI (1934), 758–771; M. B. Whiting, "The learned and virtuous Lady Bacon," *Hibbert Journal,* XXIX (1931), 270–283.

[88] C. S. Lewis, *English Literature in the Sixteenth Century* (Oxford, 1954), p. 307.

minor instances I have used the text as it appears in the *Defence,* believing that there Jewel was correcting errors which were not necessarily committed by Lady Bacon. To a certain extent the printers must be held responsible for some of the minor errors. Secretary Cecil complained that the Latin book was "negligently printed." [89] Jewel urged Parker to stop the printer, Reginald Wolf, from issuing another printing of the same book "until the said book may be better perused either by your Grace, or by some other. For in the first edition the author was many ways put to wrong; whereof these printers have small regard, as tendering only their private gain." [90] Later he wrote, "I am afraid of printers: their tyranny is terrible." [91] I feel justified, therefore, in the few corrections I have made, for they are really Jewel's corrections and not mine.

Besides the 1564 edition, I have relied heavily upon John Ayre's reproduction of it in the third volume of the Parker Society edition of Jewel's *Works.* While I have endeavored to track down every reference in the *Apology* for myself, the task has been made simpler by Ayre's prior work contained in useful if at times needlessly abbreviated footnotes. I have not attempted to specify a particular edition of a work referred to by Jewel. The person who wishes this kind of knowledge may refer to the Parker Society volume. Nevertheless, the footnotes contained in this edition are intended for the scholar as well as the general reader. For the general reader I have attempted to identify names and titles which are obscure and not a part of general knowledge in our day. For the scholar I have used Jewel's marginal references and have attempted to expand and clarify them so that specific passages may be located in the works referred to by Jewel. Where it adds nothing, I have not reproduced the marginal notes, which Jewel himself testifies were not his own.[92] I have retained these where it has been necessary to do so. The editor's notes are contained within brackets.

[89] Parker, p. 162. [90] Jewel, *Works,* IV, 1274. [91] *Ibid.,* p. 1275.
[92] *Ibid.,* p. 636.

# An Apology or Answer in Defence of the Church of England, with a Brief and Plain Declaration of the True Religion Professed and Used in the Same

(1564)

By JOHN JEWEL

## To the Right Honorable, learned and virtuous Lady A[nn] B[acon], M[atthew] C[antuar] wisheth from God grace, honor, and felicity

MADAM,

According to your request I have perused your studious labor of translation profitably employed in a right commendable work, whereof for that it liked you to make me a judge, and for that the thing itself hath singularly pleased my judgment and delighted my mind in reading it, I have right heartily to thank your ladyship, both for your own well-thinking of me and for the comfort that it hath wrought me. But, far above these private respects, I am by greater causes enforced, not only to show my rejoice of this your doing, but also to testify the same by this my writing prefixed before the work, to the commodity of others and good encouragement of yourself.

You have used your accustomed modesty in submitting it to judgment; but therein is your praise doubled, sith it hath passed judgment without reproach. And, whereas both the chief author of the Latin work and I, severally perusing and conferring your whole translation, have without alteration allowed of it, I must both desire your ladyship and advertise the readers to think that we have not therein given anything to any dissembling affection toward you, as being contented to wink at faults to please you or to make you without cause to please yourself; for there be sundry respects to draw us from so doing, although we were so evil-minded, as there is no cause why we should be so thought of. Your own judgment in discerning flattery, your modesty in misliking it, the laying open of our opinion to the world, the truth of our friendship toward you, the unwillingness of us both (in respect of our vocations) to have this public work not truly and well translated, are good causes to persuade that our allowance is of sincere truth and understanding. By which your travail, Madam, you have expressed an acceptable duty to the glory of God, deserved well of this church of Christ, honorably defended the good fame and estimation of your own native tongue, showing it so able to contend with a work originally written in the most praised speech; and, besides the honor ye have done to the kind of women and to the degree of ladies, ye have done pleasure to the author of the Latin book in delivering him by your clear translation from the perils of ambiguous and doubtful constructions and in making his good work more publicly beneficial; whereby ye have raised up great comfort to your friends and have furnished your own conscience joyfully with the fruit of your labor in so occupying your time, which must needs redound to the encouragement of noble youth in their good education, and to spend their time and knowledge in godly exercise, having delivered them by you so singular a precedent. Which your doing good, Madam, as God (I am sure) does accept and will bless with increase, so your and ours most virtuous and learned sovereign lady and mistress shall see good cause to commend; and all noble gentlewomen shall (I trust) hereby be allured from vain delights to doings of more perfect glory. And I for my part (as occasion may serve) shall exhort other to take profit by your work and follow your example, whose success I beseech our heavenly Father to bless and prosper. And now to the end both to acknowledge my good approbation and to spread the benefit more largely, where your ladyship hath sent me your book written, I have with most hearty thanks returned it to you (as you see) printed; knowing that I have therein done the best, and in this point used a reasonable policy, that is, to prevent such excuses as your modesty would have made in stay of publishing it. And thus at this time I leave further to trouble your good ladyship.

M[ATTHEW] P[ARKER]

# Part I

IT hath been an old complaint, even from the first time of the patriarchs and prophets, and confirmed by the writings and testimonies of every age, that the truth wandereth here and there as a stranger in the world and doth readily find enemies and slanderers amongst those that know her not.[1] Albeit perchance this may seem unto some a thing hard to be believed, I mean to such as have scant well and narrowly taken heed thereunto, specially seeing all mankind of nature's very motion without a teacher doth covet the truth of their own accord; and seeing our Saviour Christ himself, when he was on earth, would be called "the truth," as by a name most fit to express all his divine power; yet we—which have been exercised in the Holy Scriptures, and which have both read and seen what hath happened to all godly men commonly at all times; what to the prophets, to the apostles, to the holy martyrs, and what to Christ himself; with what rebukes, revilings, and despites they were continually vexed whiles they here lived, and that only for the truth's sake—we (I say) do see that this is not only no new thing or hard to be believed, but that it is a thing already received and commonly used from age to age. Nay, truly, this might seem much rather a marvel and beyond all belief,

[1] [Tertullian (ca. 160–ca. 220, North African church father), *Apology*, ch. i.]

if the devil, who is "the father of lies" [2] and enemy to all truth, would now upon a sudden change his nature and hope that truth might otherwise be suppressed than by belying it, or that he would begin to establish his own kingdom by using now any other practices than the same which he hath ever used from the beginning. For since any man's remembrance we can scant find one time, either when religion did first grow, or when it was settled, or when it did afresh spring up again, wherein truth and innocency were not by all unworthy means and most despitefully entreated. Doubtless the devil well seeth that so long as truth is in good safety, himself cannot be safe nor yet maintain his own estate.

For, letting pass the ancient patriarchs and prophets, who, as we said, had no part of their life free from contumelies and slanders, we know there were certain in times past which said and commonly preached that the old ancient Jews (of whom we make no doubt but they were the worshipers of the only and true God) did worship either a sow or an ass in God's stead, and that all the same religion was nothing else but a sacrilege and a plain contempt of all godliness.[3] We know also that the Son of God, our Saviour Jesus Christ, when he taught the truth, was counted a juggler [4] and an enchanter, a Samaritan, Beelzebub, a deceiver of the people, a drunkard, and a glutton.[5] Again, who wotteth [6] not what words were spoken against St. Paul, the most earnest and vehement preacher and maintainer of the truth? Sometime, that he was a seditious and busy man, a raiser of tumults, a causer of rebellion; sometime again, that he was an heretic; sometime, that he was mad. Sometime, that only upon strife and stomach he was both a blasphemer of God's law and a despiser of the fathers' ordinances. Further,

[2] [John 8:44.]

[3] [Cornelius Tacitus (ca. 55–120, pagan Roman historian), *Histories,* bk. V, ch. v.]

[4] [The word "juggler" here denotes a magician or a conjurer.]

[5] [Mark 11:19.]

[6] [I.e., knoweth.]

who knoweth not how St. Stephen, after he had throughly and sincerely embraced the truth, and began frankly and stoutly to preach and set forth the same, as he ought to do, was immediately called to answer for his life, as one that had wickedly uttered disdainful and heinous words against the Law, against Moses, against the temple, and against God? [7] Or who is ignorant that in times past there were some which reproved the Holy Scriptures of falsehood, saying they contained things both contrary and quite one against another, and how that the apostles of Christ did severally disagree betwixt themselves and that St. Paul did vary from them all? [8] And, not to make rehearsal of all, for that were an endless labor, who knoweth not after what sort our fathers were railed upon in times past, which first began to acknowledge and profess the name of Christ,[9] how they made private conspiracies, devised secret counsels against the commonwealth, and to that end made early and privy meetings in the dark, killed young babes, fed themselves with men's flesh, and, like savage and brute beasts, did drink their blood? [10] In conclusion, how that, after they had put out the candles, they committed adultery between themselves, and without regard wrought incest one with another, that brethren lay with their sisters, sons with their mothers, without any reverence of nature or kin, without shame, without difference; and that they were wicked men without all care of religion and without any opinion of God, being the very enemies of mankind, unworthy to be suffered in the world and unworthy of life?

All these things were spoken in those days against the people

[7] [Acts 6:11.]

[8] [Tertullian, *Adversus Marcionem,* bk. I, ch. xix, and bk. IV, ch. iii; Lactantius (ca. 240–ca. 320, Christian apologist and Ciceronian), *Divine Institutes,* bk. V, ch. ii.]

[9] [Eusebius (ca. 260–ca. 340, Bishop of Caesarea), *Church History,* bk. V, ch. i.]

[10] Tertull. in Apologe 3. Idem 1. 2. 3. et 7. 8. 9. [Cf. Tertullian, *Apology,* ch. ii.]

of God, against Christ Jesus, against Paul, against Stephen, and against all them, whosoever they were, which at the first beginning embraced the truth of the Gospel and were contented to be called by the name of Christians, which was then an hateful name among the common people.[11] And, although the things which they said were not true, yet the devil thought it should be sufficient for him if at the least he could bring it so to pass as they might be believed for true, and that the Christians might be brought into a common hatred of everybody and have their death and destruction sought of all sorts. Hereupon kings and princes, being led then by such persuasions, killed all the prophets of God, letting none escape—Isaiah with a saw, Jeremiah with stones, Daniel with lions, Amos with an iron bar, Paul with the sword and Christ upon the cross—and condemned all Christians to imprisonments, to torments, to the pikes, to be thrown down headlong from rocks and steep places, to be cast to wild beasts, and to be burnt; and made great fires of their quick bodies, for the only purpose to give light by night, and for a very scorn and mocking-stock; and did count them no better than the vilest filth, the offscourings and laughing-games of the whole world.[12] Thus (as ye see) have the authors and professors of the truth ever been entreated.

Wherefore we ought to bear it more quietly, which have taken upon us to profess the Gospel of Christ, if we for the same cause be handled after the same sort; and if we, as our forefathers were long ago, be likewise at this day tormented and baited with railings, with spiteful dealings, and with lies; and that for no desert of our own but only because we teach and acknowledge the truth.

They cry out upon us at this present everywhere that we are all heretics and have with new persuasions and wicked learning

[11] [*Ibid.*, ch. iii.]

[12] Suetoni in Tranquill. *In Nerone.* [Cf. Suetonius (second-century Roman historian), *Nero*, ch. xvi.]

utterly dissolved the concord of the church; that we renew, and, as it were, fetch again from hell the old and many-a-day condemned heresies; that we sow abroad new sects and such broils as never erst [13] were heard of; also that we are already divided into contrary parts and opinions and could yet by no means agree well among ourselves; that we be cursed creatures and like the giants do war against God himself and live clean without any regard or worshiping of God; that we despise all good deeds; that we use no discipline of virtue, no laws, no customs; that we esteem neither right, nor order, nor equity, nor justice; that we give the bridle to all naughtiness and provoke the people to all licentiousness and lust; that we labor and seek to overthrow the state of monarchies and kingdoms and to bring all things under the rule of the rash inconstant people and unlearned multitude; that we have seditiously fallen from the catholic church and by a wicked schism and division have shaken the whole world and troubled the common peace and universal quiet of the church; and that, as Dathan and Abiram conspired in times past against Moses and Aaron,[14] even so we at this day have renounced the Bishop of Rome without any cause reasonable; that we set nought by the authority of the ancient fathers and councils of old time; that we have rashly and presumptuously disannulled the old ceremonies, which have been well allowed by our fathers and forefathers many hundred years past, both by good customs and also in ages of more purity; and that we have by our own private head, without the authority of any sacred and general council, brought new traditions into the church; and have done all these things not for religion's sake but only upon a desire of contention and strife: but that they for their part have changed no manner of thing but have held and kept still such a number of years to this very day all things as they were delivered from the apostles and well approved by the most ancient fathers.

[13] [I.e., of old.] [14] [Numbers 16.]

And that this matter should not seem to be done but upon privy slander, and to be tossed to and fro in a corner, only to spite us, there have been besides wilily procured by the Bishop of Rome certain persons of eloquence enough, and not unlearned neither, which should put their help to this cause, now almost despaired of, and should polish and set forth the same, both in books and with long tales, to the end that when the matter was trimly and eloquently handled ignorant and unskillful persons might suspect there was some great thing in it. Indeed they perceived that their own cause did everywhere go to wrack; that their sleights were now espied and less esteemed; and that their helps did daily fail them; and that their matter stood altogether in great need of a cunning spokesman.

Now, as for those things which by them have been laid against us, in part they be manifestly false, and condemned so by their own judgments which spake them; partly again, though they be as false too indeed, yet bear they a certain show and color of truth, so as the reader (if he take not good heed) may easily be tripped and brought into error by them, specially when their fine and cunning tale is added thereunto; and part of them be of such sort as we ought not to shun them as crimes or faults but to acknowledge and profess them as things well done and upon very good reason.

For, shortly to say the truth, these folk falsely accuse and slander all our doings, yea, the same things which they themselves cannot deny but to be rightly and orderly done, and for malice do so misconstrue and deprave all our sayings and doings, as though it were impossible that any thing could be rightly spoken or done by us. They should more plainly and sincerely have gone to work if they would have dealt truly. But now they neither truly, nor sincerely, nor yet Christianly, but darkly and craftily, charge and batter us with lies and do abuse the blindness and fondness of the people, together with the ignorance of princes, to cause us to be hated and the truth to be suppressed.

This, lo ye, is the power of darkness and of men which lean more to the amazed wondering of the rude multitude and to darkness than they do to the truth and light; and, as St. Jerome saith, which do openly gainsay the truth, closing up their eyes, and will not see for the nonce.[15] But we give thanks to the most good and mighty God that such is our cause, whereagainst (when they would fainest) they were able to utter no despite but the same which might as well be wrested against the holy fathers, against the prophets, against the apostles, against Peter, against Paul, and against Christ himself.

Now therefore, if it be leefull [16] for these folks to be eloquent and fine-tongued in speaking evil, surely it becometh not us in our cause, being so very good, to be dumb in answering truly. For men to be careless what is spoken by them and their own matter, be it never so falsely and slanderously spoken (especially when it is such that the majesty of God and the cause of religion may thereby be damaged), is the part doubtless of dissolute and reckless persons and of them which wickedly wink at the injuries done unto the name of God. For, although other wrongs, yea, oftentimes great, may be borne and dissembled of a mild and Christian man; yet he that goeth smoothly away and dissembleth the matter when he is noted of heresy, Rufinus was wont to deny that man to be a Christian.[17] We therefore will do the same thing, which all laws, which nature's own voice, doth command to be done, and which Christ himself did in like case, when he was checked and reviled; to the intent we may put off from us

[15] [Jerome (ca. 342–420, biblical scholar and controversialist), *Contra Rufinum,* bk. II. This is the work to which reference is made in Jewel's *Defence.* Cf. Jewel, *Works,* III, 181.]

[16] [I.e., lawful.]

[17] [Cf. Tyrannius Rufinus (ca. 345–410, priest of Aquileia, translator of the Greek fathers into Latin), *Apologiae in S. Hieronymum,* bk. I.]

these men's slanderous accusations and may defend soberly and truly our own cause and innocency.

For Christ, verily, when the Pharisees charged him with sorcery, as one that had some familiar spirits and wrought many things by their help: "I," said he, "have not the devil, but do glorify my Father; but it is you that have dishonored me and put me to rebuke and shame." [18] And St. Paul, when Festus the lieutenant scorned him as a madman: "I," said he, "most dear Festus, am not mad, as thou thinkest, but I speak the words of truth and soberness." [19] And the ancient Christians, when they were slandered to the people for man-killers, for adulterers, for committers of incest, for disturbers of commonweals, and did perceive that by such slanderous accusations the religion which they professed might be brought in question, namely, if they should seem to hold their peace and in manner confess the fault; lest this might hinder the free course of the Gospel, they made orations, they put up supplications, and made means to emperors and princes that they might defend themselves and their fellows in open audience.

But we, truly, seeing that so many thousands of our brethren in these last twenty years have borne witness unto the truth in the midst of most painful torments that could be devised; and when princes, desirous to restrain the Gospel, sought many ways, but prevailed nothing; and that now almost the whole world doth begin to open their eyes to behold the light; we take it that our cause hath already been sufficiently declared and defended, and think it not needful to make many words, since the very matter saith enough for itself. For, if the Popes would, or else if they could, weigh with their own selves the whole matter, and also the beginning and proceedings of our religion, how in a manner all their travail hath come to nought, nobody driving it forward, and without any worldly help; and how, on the other side, our cause, against the will of emperors from

[18] [John 8:49.] [19] [Acts 26:25.]

the beginning, against the wills of so many kings, in spite of the Popes, and almost mauger [20] the head of all men, hath taken increase, and by little and little spread over into all countries, and is come at length even into kings' courts and palaces. These same things, methinketh, might be tokens great enough to them that God himself doth strongly fight in our quarrel and doth from heaven laugh at their enterprises; and that the force of the truth is such as neither man's power nor yet hell gates are able to root it out. For they be not all mad at this day, so many free cities, so many kings, so many princes, which have fallen away from the seat of Rome and have rather joined themselves to the Gospel of Christ.

And, although the Popes have never hitherunto leisure to consider diligently and earnestly of these matters, or though some other cares do now let [21] them and diverse ways pull them, or though they count these to be but common and trifling studies and nothing to appertain to the Pope's worthiness, this maketh not why our matter ought to seem the worse. Or if they perchance will not see that which they see indeed, but rather will withstand the known truth, ought we therefore by and by to be counted heretics, because we obey not their will and pleasure? If so be that Pope Pius were the man (we say not, which he would so gladly be called), but if he were indeed a man that either would account us for his brethren, or at least would take us to be men, he would first diligently have examined our reasons and would have seen what might be said with us, what against us, and would not in his bull, whereby he lately pretended a council,[22] so rashly have condemned so great a part of the world, so many learned and godly men, so many commonwealths, so many kings, and so many princes, only upon his own blind

[20] [I.e., in spite of.] [21] [I.e., hinder.]

[22] [By means of a papal bull issued on November 29, 1560, Pope Pius IV summoned the third meeting of the Council of Trent to begin on April 6, 1561. Actually the first session was held on January 18, 1562.]

prejudices and foredeterminations, and that without hearing of them speak, or without showing cause why.

But because he hath already so noted us openly, lest by holding our peace we should seem to grant a fault, and specially because we can by no means have audience in the public assembly of the general council, wherein he would no creature should have power to give his voice or declare his opinion except he were sworn and straitly bound to maintain his authority—for we have had experience hereof in the last conference at the Council of Trent, where the ambassadors and divines of the princes of Germany and of the free cities were quite shut out from their company; neither can we yet forget how Julius the Third,[23] above ten years past, provided warily by his writ that none of our sort should be suffered to speak in the Council (except that there were some man peradventure that would recant and change his opinion)—for this cause chiefly we thought it good to yield up an account of our faith in writing and truly and openly to make answer to those things wherewith we have been openly charged; to the end the world may see the parts and foundations of that doctrine in the behalf whereof so many good men have little regarded their own lives; and that all men may understand what manner of people they be, and what opinion they have of God and of religion, whom the Bishop of Rome, before they were called to tell their tale, hath condemned for heretics, without any good consideration, without any example, and utterly without law or right, only because he heard tell that they did dissent from him and his in some point of religion.

And although St. Jerome would have nobody to be patient when he is suspected of heresy,[24] yet we will deal herein neither

[23] [Pope Julius III reigned in Rome during the second meeting of the Council of Trent (1551–1552).]

[24] [John Ayre, editor of Jewel's *Works,* suggests that this comes from Jerome's letter to Pammachium against the errors of John of Jerusalem. Cf. Jewel, *Works,* III, 209.]

bitterly nor brabblingly,[25] nor yet be carried away with anger and heat, though he ought to be reckoned neither bitter nor brabbler that speaketh the truth. We willingly leave this kind of eloquence to our adversaries, who, whatsoever they say against us, be it never so shrewdly or despitefully said, yet think it is said modestly and comely enough and care nothing whether it be true or false. We need none of these shifts, which do maintain the truth.

Further, if we do show it plain that God's Holy Gospel, the ancient bishops, and the primitive church do make on our side, and that we have not without just cause left these men, and rather have returned to the apostles and old catholic fathers; and if we shall be found to do the same not colorably or craftily but in good faith before God, truly, honestly, clearly, and plainly; and if they themselves which fly our doctrine and would be called catholics shall manifestly see how all these titles of antiquity, whereof they boast so much, are quite shaken out of their hands, and that there is more pith in this our cause than they thought for; we then hope and trust that none of them will be so negligent and careless of his own salvation but he will at length study and bethink himself to whether part he were best to join him. Undoubtedly, except one will altogether harden his heart and refuse to hear, he shall not repent him to give good heed to this our defense, and to mark well what we say and how truly and justly it agreeth with Christian religion.

For where they call us heretics, it is a crime so heinous, that, unless it may be seen, unless it may be felt, and in manner may be holden with hands and fingers, it ought not lightly to be judged or believed, when it is laid to the charge of any Christian man. For heresy is a forsaking of salvation, a renouncing of God's grace, a departing from the body and spirit of Christ. But this was ever an old and solemn property with them and

[25] [I.e., clamorously.]

their forefathers, if any did complain of their errors and faults and desired to have true religion restored, straightway to condemn such ones for heretics, as men newfangled and factious. Christ for no other cause was called a Samaritan but only for that he was thought to have fallen to a certain new religion and to be the author of a new sect. And Paul, the apostle of Christ, was called before the judges to make answer to a matter of heresy, and therefore he said: "According to this way, which they call heresy, I do worship the God of my fathers; believing all things which be written in the Law and in the prophets." [26]

Shortly to speak, this universal religion, which Christian men profess at this day, was called first of the heathen people a sect and heresy.[27] With these terms did they always fill princes' ears, to the intent when they had once hated us with a foredetermined opinion and had counted all that we said to be faction and heresy, they might be so led away from the truth and right understanding of the cause.[28] But the more sore and outrageous a crime heresy is, the more it ought to be proved by plain and strong arguments, especially in this time, when men begin to give less credit to their words and to make more diligent search of their doctrine than they were wont to do. For the people of God are otherwise instructed now than they were in times past, when all the Bishop of Rome's sayings were allowed for gospel, and when all religion did depend only upon their authority. Nowadays the Holy Scripture is abroad, the writings of the apostles and prophets are in print, whereby all truth and catholic doctrine may be proved and all heresy may be disproved and confuted.

Sithence, then, they bring forth none of these for themselves, and call us nevertheless heretics which have neither fallen from Christ, nor from the apostles, nor yet from the prophets,

[26] [Acts 24:14.]  [27] Tertull. in Apologetico. [Cf. ch. x.]

[28] [The preceding three sentences were omitted in Harding's *Confutation* and Jewel's *Defence*.]

this is an injurious and a very spiteful dealing. With this sword did Christ put off the devil when he was tempted of him; with these weapons ought all presumption, which doth advance itself against God, to be overthrown and conquered. "For all Scripture," saith St. Paul, "that cometh by the inspiration of God, is profitable to teach, to confute, to instruct, and to reprove; that the man of God may be perfect, and throughly framed to every good work." [29] Thus did the holy fathers always fight against the heretics with none other force than with the Holy Scriptures. St. Augustine, when he disputed against Petilian, an heretic of the Donatists: [30] "Let not these words," quod he, "be heard between us, 'I say' or 'you say': let us rather speak in this wise: 'Thus saith the Lord.' There let us seek the church: there let us boult [31] out our cause." [32] Likewise St. Jerome: "All those things," saith he, "which without the testimony of the Scriptures are holden as delivered from the apostles be throughly smitten down by the sword of God's word." [33] St. Ambrose also, to Gratian the emperor: "Let the Scripture," saith he, "be asked the question, let the apostles be asked, let the prophets be asked, and let Christ be asked." [34] For at that time made the catholic fathers and bishops no doubt but that our religion might be proved out of the Holy Scriptures. Neither were they ever so hardy to take any for an heretic whose error

[29] [II Tim. 3:16–17.]

[30] [The Donatists were schismatics in North Africa, beginning in 311 with their rejection of Caecilian, who was consecrated Bishop of Carthage in that year.]

[31] [I.e., examine.]

[32] [Augustine (354–430, Bishop of Hippo Regius, one of the great theologians of the church), *Epistola ad catholicos contra Donatistas, vulgo de unitate ecclesiae,* ch. iii.] Et contra Maximinum Arianorum Episcop. li. 3. cap. 14. [Augustine, *Contra Maximinum haereticum Arianorum episcopum,* bk. II, ch. xiv.]

[33] In primum capus Aggae. [Not found in place indicated. Cf. Jerome, *Breviarium in Psalmos,* Ps. lxxxvi.]

[34] [Cf. Ambrose (ca. 339–397, Bishop of Milan, "Doctor of the Church"), *De fide,* bk. I, ch. vi.]

they could not evidently and apparently reprove by the selfsame Scriptures. And we verily do make answer on this wise, as St. Paul did, "According to this way which they call heresy we do worship God and the Father of our Lord Jesus Christ, and do allow all things which have been written either in the Law, or in the prophets," [35] or in the apostles' works.

Wherefore, if we be heretics, and they (as they would fain be called) be catholics, why do they not as they see the fathers, which were catholic men, have always done? Why do they not convince and master us by the divine Scriptures? Why do they not call us again to be tried by them? Why do they not lay before us how we have gone away from Christ, from the prophets, from the apostles, and from the holy fathers? Why stick they to do it? Why are they afraid of it? It is God's cause: why are they doubtful to commit it to the trial of God's word? If we be heretics, which refer all our controversies unto the Holy Scriptures and report us to the selfsame words which we know were sealed by God himself, and in comparison of them set little by all other things, whatsoever may be devised by men; how shall we say to these folk, I pray you, what manner of men be they, and how is it meet to call them, which fear the judgment of the Holy Scriptures, that is to say, the judgment of God himself, and do prefer before them their own dreams and full cold inventions; and, to maintain their own traditions, have defaced and corrupted, now these many hundred years, the ordinances of Christ and of the apostles?

Men say that Sophocles, the tragical poet, when in his old days he was by his own sons accused before the judges for a doting and sottish man, as one that fondly wasted his own substance and seemed to need a governor to see unto him; to the intent he might clear himself of the fault, he came into the place of judgment, and, when he had rehearsed before them his tragedy called *Oedipus Coloneus*, which he had written

[35] [Acts 24:14.]

at the very time of his accusation, marvelous exactly and cunningly, did of himself ask the judges whether they thought any sottish or doting man could do the like piece of work.

In like manner, because these men take us to be mad and appeach us for heretics, as men which have nothing to do neither with Christ nor with the church of God; we have judged it should be to good purpose and not unprofitable if we do openly and frankly set forth our faith wherein we stand and show all that confidence which we have in Christ Jesus, to the intent all men may see what is our judgment of every part of Christian religion and may resolve with themselves whether the faith which they shall see confirmed by the words of Christ, by the writings of the apostles, by the testimonies of the catholic fathers, and by the examples of many ages, be but a certain rage of furious and mad men and a conspiracy of heretics. This therefore is our belief.

# Part II

WE believe that there is one certain nature and divine power which we call God; and that the same is divided into three equal Persons—into the Father, into the Son, and into the Holy Ghost; and that they all be of one power, of one majesty, of one eternity, of one Godhead, and of one substance. And, although these three Persons be so divided that neither the Father is the Son, nor the Son is the Holy Ghost or the Father; yet nevertheless we believe that there is but one very God and that the same one God has created heaven, and earth, and all things contained under heaven.

We believe that Jesus Christ, the only Son of the eternal Father (as long before it was determined before all beginnings), when the fullness of time was come, did take of that blessed and pure Virgin both flesh and all the nature of man, that he might declare to the world the secret and hid will of his Father, which will had been laid up from before all ages and generations; and that he might full finish in his human body the mystery of our redemption; and might fasten to the cross our sins and also that handwriting which was made against us.

We believe that for our sakes he died and was buried, descended into hell, the third day by the power of his Godhead returned to life and rose again; and that the fortieth day after his resurrection, whiles his disciples beheld and looked upon him, he ascended into heaven, to fulfill all things, and did place in majesty and glory the selfsame body wherewith he was born, wherein he lived on earth, wherein he was jested at, wherein he had suffered most painful torments and cruel kind of death, wherein he rose again, and wherein he ascended to the right hand of the Father,[1] "above all rule, above all power, all force, all dominion, and above every name which is named, not only in this world, but also in the world to come"; and that there he now sitteth, and shall sit, till all things be full perfected.[2] And, although the majesty and Godhead of Christ be everywhere abundantly dispersed, yet we believe that his body, as St. Augustine saith, "must needs be still in one place"; and that Christ hath given majesty unto his body, but yet hath not taken away from it the nature of a body; and that we must not so affirm Christ to be God that we deny him to be man; [3] and, as the martyr Vigilius saith, that "Christ hath left us as touching his human nature, but hath not left us as touching his divine nature"; [4] and that the same Christ, though he be absent from us concerning his manhood, yet is ever present with us concerning his Godhead. From that place also we believe that Christ shall come again to execute that general judgment, as well of them whom he shall then find alive in the body as of them that be already dead.[5]

We believe that the Holy Ghost, who is the third Person in the Holy Trinity, is very God; not made, not created, not begotten, but proceeding from both the Father and the Son, by a certain mean unknown unto men and unspeakable; and that it is his property to mollify and soften the hardness of man's heart, when he is once received thereunto, either by the whole-

[1] [Augustine, *In Joannis Euangelium,* tractatus 50, sec. 13.]

[2] [Acts 3:21.]

[3] In Epist. ad Dardanum. [Augustine, *Epist.* 187, ch. iii.]

[4] [Vigilius (ca. 500, Bishop of Thapsus), *Contra Eutychetem,* bk. I.]

[5] [Fulgentius (468–533, Bishop of Ruspe in North Africa), *Ad Thrasimundum vandalorum,* bk. II, ch. xvii.]

some preaching of the Gospel, or by any other way; that he doth give men light, and guide them unto the knowledge of God, to all way of truth, to newness of the whole life, and to everlasting hope of salvation.

We believe that there is one church of God, and that the same is not shut up (as in times past among the Jews) into some one corner or kingdom, but that it is catholic and universal and dispersed throughout the whole world. So that there is now no nation which can truly complain that they be shut forth and may not be one of the church and people of God. And that this church is the kingdom, the body, and the spouse of Christ; and that Christ alone is the prince of this kingdom; that Christ alone is the head of this body; and that Christ alone is the bridegroom of this spouse.

Furthermore, (we believe) that there be divers degrees of ministers in the church, whereof some be deacons, some priests, some bishops, to whom is committed the office to instruct the people and the whole charge and setting forth of religion. Yet notwithstanding we say that there neither is nor can be any one man which may have the whole superiority in this universal state; for that Christ is ever present to assist his church and needeth not any man to supply his room as his only heir to all his substance; and that there can be no one mortal creature which is able to comprehend or conceive in his mind the universal church, that is to wit, all parts of the world, much less able to put them in order and to govern them rightly and duly. For all the apostles, as Cyprian saith, were of like power among themselves, and the rest were the same that Peter was;[6] and that it was said indifferently to them all, "Feed ye"; indifferently to them all, "Go into the whole world"; indifferently to them all, "Teach ye the Gospel." And as Jerome saith, "All bishops wheresoever they be, be they at Rome, be they at Eugubium, be

[6] De Simplic. praelat. [Cyprian (third-century Bishop of Carthage), *De unitate ecclesiae,* 2nd ed., ch. iv.]

they at Constantinople, be they at Rhegium, be all of like preeminence and of like priesthood."[7] And, as Cyprian saith, "There is but one bishopric, and a piece thereof is perfectly and wholly holden of every particular bishop."[8] And, according to the judgment of the Nicene council,[9] we say that the Bishop of Rome has no more jurisdiction over the church of God than the rest of the patriarchs, either of Alexandria or Antioch, have. And as for the Bishop of Rome, who now calleth all matters before himself alone, except he do his duty as he ought to do, except he administer the sacraments, except he instruct the people, except he warn them and teach them, we say that he ought not of right once to be called a bishop, or so much as an elder. For a bishop, as saith Augustine, "is a name of labor, and not of honor";[10] because he would have that man understand himself to be no bishop which will seek to have preeminence, and not to profit others. And that neither the Pope, nor any other worldly creature, can no more be head of the whole church, or a bishop over all, than he can be the bridegroom, the light, the salvation, and the life of the church. For these privileges and names belong only to Christ, and be properly and only fit for him alone. And that no Bishop of Rome did ever suffer himself to be called by such a proud name and title before Phocas the Emperor's time, who, as we know, by killing his own sovereign, Maurice the Emperor, did by a traitorous villainy aspire to the empire, which was about the sixth hundred and thirteenth year after Christ was born. And the Council of

[7] [Jerome, *Epist. ad Euagrium* (Euagrius Ponticus, church writer, preacher, monk of the fourth century). See Erasmus' interpretation of this letter in *Hieronymi operum* (Basle, 1553), II, 330.]

[8] De Simpli. Praelatorum. [Cyprian, *De unitate ecclesiae,* ch. v.]

[9] [Reference is made here to the Council of Nicaea, Canon 6. This was the first of the general councils of the early church that were considered authoritative by Jewel. The first four general councils are Nicaea (325), Constantinople (381), Ephesus (431), and Chalcedon (451).]

[10] [Augustine, *De civitate Dei,* bk. XIX, ch. xix.]

Carthage did circumspectly provide that no bishop should be called either the highest bishop or chief priest.[11]

And therefore, sithence the Bishop of Rome will nowadays so be called, and challengeth unto himself an authority that is none of his, besides that he doth plainly contrary to the ancient councils and contrary to the old fathers, we believe that he does give unto himself, as it is written by his own companion Gregory, a presumptuous, a profane, a sacrilegious, and an Antichristian name; that he is also the king of pride; that he is Lucifer, which preferreth himself before his brethren; that he has forsaken the faith, and is the forerunner of Antichrist.[12]

Further, we say that the minister ought lawfully, duly, and orderly to be preferred to that office of the church of God, and that no man hath power to wrest himself into the holy ministry at his own pleasure and list. Wherefore these persons do us the greater wrong which have nothing so common in their mouth as that we do nothing orderly and comely but all things troublesomely and without order; and that we allow every man to be a priest, to be a teacher, and to be an interpreter of the Scriptures.

Moreover, we say that Christ hath given to his ministers power to bind, to loose, to open, to shut; and that the office of loosing consisteth in this point, that the minister either by the preaching of the Gospel offers the merits of Christ and full pardon to such as have lowly and contrite hearts and do unfeignedly repent them, pronouncing unto the same a sure and undoubted forgiveness of their sins and hope of everlasting salvation; or else that the same minister, when any have offended their brothers' minds with some great offense or notable and open crime, whereby they have, as it were, banished and made

[11] Ca. 47. [Cf. Petro Crabbe, *Concilia* (Cologne, 1551), I, 428, Council of Carthage, III, ch. xxvi.]

[12] Gregor. epistola li. 4. epist. 76, 78, 80. Et lib. 7. epist. 66. [Cf. Gregory the Great (Bishop of Rome from 590), various letters as enumerated by John Ayre in Jewel, *Works*, I, 344–345.]

themselves strangers from the common fellowship and from the body of Christ, then, after perfect amendment of such persons, doth reconcile them, and bring them home again, and restore them to the company and unity of the faithful. We say also that the minister doth execute the authority of binding and shutting as often as he shutteth up the gate of the kingdom of heaven against the unbelieving and stubborn persons, denouncing unto them God's vengeance and everlasting punishment, or else, when he doth quite shut them out from the bosom of the church by open excommunication. Out of doubt, what sentence soever the minister of God shall give in this sort, God himself doth so well allow of it that whatsoever here in earth by their means is loosed and bound God himself will loose and bind the same in heaven.

And touching the keys wherewith they may either shut or open the kingdom of heaven, we with Chrysostom say they be "the knowledge of the Scriptures": [13] with Tertullian we say they be "the interpretation of the Law"; [14] and with Eusebius we call them "the word of God."

Moreover, that Christ's disciples did receive this authority, not that they should hear private confessions of the people and listen to their whisperings, as the common Massing priests do everywhere nowadays, and do it so as though in that one point lay all the virtue and use of the keys; but to the end they should go, they should teach, they should publish abroad the Gospel, and be unto the believing a sweet savor of life unto life, and unto the unbelieving and unfaithful a savor of death unto death; and that the minds of godly persons, being brought low by the remorse of their former life and errors, after they once begun to look up unto the light of the Gospel and believe in Christ,

[13] [Cf. John Chrysostom (fourth-century Bishop of Constantinople, theologian and preacher), *Opus imperfectum in Matthaeum,* homilia xliv, ch. xxiii. This is not considered a genuine work of Chrysostom.]

[14] [Tertullian, *Adversus Marcionem,* bk. IV, sec. 27.]

might be opened with the word of God, even as a door is opened with a key. Contrariwise, that the wicked and willful folk, and such as would not believe nor return into the right way, should be left still as fast locked and shut up, and, as St. Paul saith, "wax worse and worse."[15] This take we to be the meaning of the keys; and that after this fashion men's consciences be either opened or shut. We say that the priest indeed is judge in this case, but yet hath no manner of right to challenge an authority or power, as saith Ambrose.[16] And therefore our Saviour Jesus Christ, to reprove the negligence of the scribes and Pharisees in teaching, did with these words rebuke them, saying, "Woe unto you scribes and Pharisees, which have taken away the keys of knowledge and have shut up the kingdom of heaven before men."[17] Seeing then the key, whereby the way and entry to the kingdom of God is opened unto us, is the word of the Gospel and the expounding of the Law and the Scriptures, we say plainly, where the same word is not, there is not the key. And seeing one manner of word is given to all, and one only key belongeth to all, we say there is but one only power of all ministers, as concerning opening and shutting. And as touching the Bishop of Rome, for all that his parasites flatteringly sing these words in his ears, "To thee will I give the keys of the kingdom of heaven" (as though those keys were fit for him alone and for nobody else), except he go so to work as men's consciences may be made pliant and be subdued to the word of God, we deny that he doth either open, or shut, or hath the keys at all. And although he taught and instructed the people (as would to God he might once truly do and persuade himself it were at the least some piece of his duty), yet we think his key to be never a whit better or of greater force than other

[15] [II Tim. 3:13.]

[16] De poenitentia. dist. 1, cap. Verbum Dei. [Cf. Jewel, *Works*, III, 378, n. 4.]

[17] [Luke 11:52; Matt. 23:13.]

men's. For who hath severed him from the rest? Who hath taught him more cunningly to open, or better to absolve, than his brethren?

We say that matrimony is holy and honorable in all sorts and states of persons, as in the patriarchs, in the prophets, in the apostles, in holy martyrs, in the ministers of the church, and in bishops, and that it is an honest and lawful thing (as Chrysostom saith) for a man living in matrimony to take upon him therewith the dignity of a bishop.[18] And, as Sozomen saith of Spyridion,[19] and as Nazianzene saith of his own father,[20] we say that a good and diligent bishop doth serve in the ministry never the worse for that he is married, but rather the better, and with more ableness to do good. Further we say that the same law which by constraint taketh away this liberty from men and compelleth them against their wills to live single is "the doctrine of devils," as Paul saith; [21] and that, ever since the time of this law, a wonderful uncleanness of life and manners in God's ministers and sundry horrible enormities have followed, as the Bishop of Augusta, as Faber, as Abbas Panormitanus, as Latomus,[22] as the Tripartite work which is annexed to the second tome of the Councils,[23] and other champions of the Pope's band, yea, and as the matter itself and all histories do confess. For it was rightly said by Pius the Second, a Bishop of Rome,

[18] [John Chrysostom, *In epist. ad Titum,* ch. i, hom. ii.]

[19] [Sozomen (early fifth-century church historian), *Church History,* bk. I, ch. xi; Eusebius, *Church History,* bk. X, ch. v. Spyridion was the fourth-century Bishop of Tremithus in Cyprus.]

[20] Nazianzen in monodia de Basilie. [Gregory of Nazianzus (fourth-century theologian, one of the Cappadocian fathers), *Oratio XVIII, Funebris in patrem, praesente Basilio,* sec. 18.]

[21] [I Tim. 4:1–3.]

[22] [Huldericus, tenth-century Bishop of Augusta in Germany; Jacobus Faber Stapulensis (Jacques Le Fèvre d'Étaples), French humanist, d. 1536; Panormitanus, fifteenth-century Benedictine abbot.]

[23] [Cf. Crabbe, *Concilia,* II, 1002.]

that he saw many causes why wives should be taken away from priests, but that he saw many more and more weighty causes why they ought to be restored them again.[24]

We receive and embrace all the canonical Scriptures, both of the Old and New Testament, giving thanks to our God, who hath raised up unto us that light which we might ever have before our eyes, lest, either by the subtlety of men, or by the snares of the devil, we should be carried away to errors and lies. Also that these be the heavenly voices whereby God hath opened unto us his will; and that only in them man's heart can have settled rest; that in them be abundantly and fully comprehended all things, whatsoever be needful for our salvation, as Origen, Augustine, Chrysostom, and Cyril have taught; that they be the very might and strength of God to attain to salvation; that they be the foundations of the prophets and apostles whereupon is built the church of God; that they be the very sure and infallible rule whereby may be tried whether the church doth stagger or err and whereunto all ecclesiastical doctrine ought to be called to account; and that against these Scriptures neither law, nor ordinance, nor any custom ought to be heard; no, though Paul himself, or an angel from heaven, should come and teach the contrary.

Moreover, we allow the sacraments of the church, that is to say, certain holy signs and ceremonies, which Christ would we should use, that by them he might set before our eyes the mysteries of our salvation, and might more strongly confirm the faith which we have in his blood, and might seal his grace in our hearts. And these sacraments, together with Tertullian, Origen, Ambrose, Augustine, Jerome, Chrysostom, Basil, Dionysius, and other catholic fathers, do we call figures, signs, marks or badges, prints, copies, forms, seals, signets, similitudes, pat-

[24] [Bartolomeo Platina (1421–1481, Italian humanist), *De vitis et gestis summorum pontificum* (Cologne, 1551), p. 295. Pius II (1405–1464) was Aeneas Sylvius.]

terns, representations, remembrances, and memories. And we make no doubt, together with the same doctors, to say that these be certain visible words, seals of righteousness, tokens of grace; and we do expressly pronounce that in the Lord's Supper there is truly given unto the believing the body and blood of our Lord, the flesh of the Son of God, which quickeneth our souls, the meat that cometh from above, the food of immortality, of grace, truth, and life; and the same supper to be the communion of the body and blood of Christ by the partaking whereof we be revived, we be strengthened, and be fed unto immortality; and whereby we are joined, united, and incorporate unto Christ, that we may abide in him, and he in us.

Besides, we acknowledge there be two sacraments, which, we judge, properly ought to be called by this name; that is to say, baptism and the sacrament of thanksgiving. For thus many we see were delivered and sanctified by Christ, and well allowed of the old fathers, Ambrose and Augustine.

We say that baptism is a sacrament of the remission of sins and of that washing which we have in the blood of Christ; and that no person which will profess Christ's name ought to be restrained or kept back therefrom; no, not the very babes of Christians; forsomuch as they be born in sin and pertain unto the people of God.

We say that Eucharistia, the supper of the Lord, is a sacrament, that is to wit, an evident token of the body and blood of Christ, wherein is set, as it were, before our eyes the death of Christ and his resurrection, and what act soever he did whilst he was in his mortal body; to the end we may give him thanks for his death and for our deliverance; and that, by the often receiving of this sacrament, we may daily renew the remembrance of that matter, to the intent we, being fed with the body and blood of Christ, may be brought into the hope of the resurrection and of everlasting life and may most assuredly believe that the body and blood of Christ doth in like manner feed our souls, as bread and wine doth feed our bodies. To this banquet we think the people of God ought to be earnestly bidden, that they may all communicate among themselves and openly declare and testify both the godly society which is among them and also the hope which they have in Christ Jesus. For this cause, if there had been any which could be but a looker-on and abstain from the Holy Communion, him did the old fathers and Bishops of Rome in the primitive church, before private Mass came up, excommunicate as a wicked person and as a pagan.[25] Neither was there any Christian at that time which did communicate alone whiles others looked on. For so did Calixtus in times past decree that, after the consecration was finished, all should communicate, except they had rather stand without the church doors; "because thus," saith he, "did the apostles appoint, and the same the holy church of Rome keepeth still.[26]

Moreover, when the people come to the Holy Communion, the sacrament ought to be given them in both kinds; for so both Christ hath commanded and the apostles in every place have ordained, and all the ancient fathers and catholic bishops have followed the same. And whoso doth contrary to this, he (as Gelasius saith) commits sacrilege.[27] And therefore we say that our adversaries at this day, who, having violently thrust out and quite forbidden the Holy Communion, do, without the word of God, without the authority of any ancient council, without any catholic father, without any example of the primitive church, yea, and without reason also, defend and maintain their private Masses and the mangling of the sacraments, and do this not only against the plain express commandment and bidding of

[25] [Chrysostom, *In epist. ad Ephesios,* ch. i, hom. iii.]

[26] Dist. 2. Saecularea. De Cons. dist. 2. Cap. Peracta. [Cf. Jewel, *Works,* III, 472, n. 7. The Calixtus mentioned in Jewel's text was Callistus I, third-century Bishop of Rome. The Anacletus whom Jewel specified was a first-century Bishop of Rome. Jewel attributed his confusion here to Gratian, the twelfth-century canonist.]

[27] De Consecr. Dist. 2. Comperimus. [Gelasius (late fifth-century Bishop of Rome) in *Corpus juris canonici* (Paris, 1624), tom. I, Decretum Gratiani, col. 1918.]

Christ, but also against all antiquity, do wickedly therein and are very church robbers.

We affirm that bread and wine are holy and heavenly mysteries of the body and blood of Christ, and that by them Christ himself, being the true bread of eternal life, is so presently given unto us as that by faith we verily receive his body and blood. Yet say we not this so as though we thought that the very nature of bread is changed and goeth to nothing, as many have dreamed in these later times which yet could never agree among themselves upon their own dreams. For that was not Christ's meaning, that the wheaten bread should lay apart his own nature and receive a certain new divinity, but that he might rather change us, and (to use Theophylact's words) might transform us into his body.[28] For what can be said more plainly than that which Ambrose saith, "Bread and wine remain still the same they were before and yet are changed into another thing"; [29] or that which Gelasius saith, "The substance of the bread, or the nature of the wine, ceaseth not so to be"; [30] or that which Theodoret saith, "After the consecration the mystical signs do not cast off their own proper nature; for they remain still in their former substance, form, and kind"; [31] or that which Augustine saith, "That which you see is the bread and cup, and so our eyes tell us, but that which your faith requireth to be taught is this: the bread is the body of Christ, and the cup is his blood"; [32] or that which Origen saith, "Bread which is sanctified by the word of God, as touching the material substance thereof, goeth into the belly, and is cast

[28] [Theophylact (eleventh-century Byzantine biblical exegete), *In Joannis,* ch. xvi.]

[29] [Ambrose, *De sacramentis,* bk. IV, ch. iv.]

[30] [Gelasius, *Adversus Eutychetem et Nestorium* (Nestorius was a fifth-century theologian and preacher, reputedly the founder of the Nestorian heresy).]

[31] In Dialogis 1 & 2. [Theodoret (ca. 393–458, Bishop of Cyrrhus), *Inconfus. dialogis,* II.]

[32] [Augustine, Sermo 272, *Ad infantes, de sacramento;*] De Consecr. Dist. 2. cap. Qui Manducat. [The gloss on canon 48 in the *Corpus juris canonici,* Decretum Gratiani, Dist. ii.]

out into the privy";[33] or that which Christ himself said, not only after blessing of the cup, but also after he had ministered the communion: "I will drink no more of this fruit of the vine"?[34] It is well known that the fruit of the vine is wine and not blood.

And in speaking thus we mean not to abase the Lord's Supper, or to teach that it is but a cold ceremony only and nothing to be wrought therein (as many falsely slander us we teach). For we affirm that Christ does truly and presently give himself wholly in his sacraments; in baptism, that we may put him on; and in his supper, that we may eat him by faith and spirit and may have everlasting life by his cross and blood. And we say not, this is done slightly and coldly, but effectually and truly. For, although we do not touch the body of Christ with teeth and mouth, yet we hold him fast and eat him by faith, by understanding, and by spirit. And it is no vain faith which doth comprehend Christ; and that is not received with cold devotion which is received with understanding, with faith, and with spirit. For Christ himself altogether is so offered and given us in these mysteries that we may certainly know we be flesh of his flesh and bone of his bones; and that Christ continueth in us and we in him. And therefore in celebrating these mysteries, the people are to good purpose exhorted, before they come to receive the Holy Communion, to lift up their hearts and to direct their minds to heavenward; because he is there by whom we must be full fed and live.[35] Cyril saith, when we come to receive these mysteries, all gross imaginations must quite be banished.[36] The Council of Nicaea, as it is alleged by some in Greek, plainly

[33] Origene in Mat. Hom. 15. [Origen (ca. 185–254, Alexandrian exegete, theologian, teacher), *Commentaria in Euangelium Matthaeum,* tom. XI, hom. xiv.]

[34] [Mark 14:25.]

[35] De Cons. dist. 1. ca. Quando. [Cf. *Corpus juris canonici,* Decretum Gratiani, Dist. i.]

[36] Ad Objecti. Theodoreti. [This reference to the source of the statement on Cyril (Patriarch of Alexandria, 412–444) was abandoned later. Cf. Jewel, *Works,* III, 536 ff.]

forbiddeth us to be basely affectioned or bent toward the bread and wine which are set before us.[37] And, as Chrysostom very aptly writeth, we say that "the body of Christ is the dead carcass, and we ourselves must be the eagles": meaning thereby that we must fly on high if we will come unto the body of Christ. "For this table," as Chrysostom saith, "is a table of eagles, and not of jays." [38] Cyprian also, "This bread," saith he, "is food of the soul, and not the meat of the belly." [39] And Augustine, "How shall I hold him," saith he, "which is absent? How shall I reach my hand up to heaven, to lay hold upon him that sitteth there?" He answereth, "Reach thither thy faith, and then thou hast laid hold on him." [40]

We cannot also away in our churches with the shows, and sales, and buying and selling of Masses, nor the carrying about and worshiping of bread; nor such other idolatrous and blasphemous fondness which none of them can prove that Christ or his apostles did ever ordain or left unto us. And we justly blame the Bishops of Rome, who, without the word of God, without the authority of the holy fathers, without any example of antiquity, after a new guise, do not only set before the people the sacramental bread to be worshiped as God, but do also carry the same about upon an ambling horse, whithersoever themselves journey,[41] in such sort as in old time the Persians' fire and the relics of the goddess Isis were solemnly carried about in procession; and have brought the sacraments of Christ to be used now as a stage play and a solemn sight; to the end that men's eyes

[37] [Cf. Gelasius of Cyzicus (ca. 475, church historian), *Historia Concilii Nicaeni,* bk. II, ch. xxx, 7.]

[38] Chrysost. in 10 ad Corinth. [Chrysostom, *In epistolam primam ad Corinthios,* hom. xxiv.]

[39] [Jewel falsely ascribed *De coena Domini* to Cyprian. The exact words used by Jewel cannot be located.]

[40] [Augustine, *In Joannis Euangelium,* ch. xi, tract. 50, sec. 4.]

[41] In libro de Ceremoniis Romanae Ecclesiae. [*Ceremoniarum sive rituum ecclesiasticarum, Rom. Eccles.* (Cologne, 1557), bk. I, sec. 12, ch. i, fol. 108(b).]

should be fed with nothing else but with mad gazings and foolish gauds, in the selfsame matter wherein the death of Christ ought diligently to be beaten into our hearts, and wherein also the mysteries of our redemption ought with all holiness and reverence to be executed.

Besides, where they say, and sometime do persuade fools, that they are able by their Masses to distribute and apply unto men's commodity all the merits of Christ's death, yea, although many times the parties think nothing of the matter and understand full little what is done, this is a mockery, a heathenish fancy, and a very toy. For it is our faith that applieth the death and cross of Christ to our benefit, and not the act of the Massing priest. "Faith had in the sacraments," saith Augustine, "doth justify, and not the sacraments."[42] And Origen saith, "Christ is the priest, the propitiation, and sacrifice; which propitiation comes to everyone by means of faith."[43] So that by this reckoning we say that the sacraments of Christ without faith do not once profit those that be alive; a great deal less do they profit those that be dead.

And as for their brags they are wont to make of their purgatory, though we know it is not a thing so very late risen amongst them, yet is it no better than a blockish and an old wives' device.

Augustine indeed sometime saith there is such a certain place; sometime he denieth not but there may be such a one; sometime he doubts; sometime again he utterly denies it to be and thinketh that men are therein deceived by a certain natural good will they bear their friends departed.[44] But yet of this one error

[42] [Cf. Augustine, *In Joannis Euangelium,* ch. xv, tract. 80, sec. 3.]

[43] Orig. ad Rom. i. cap. 3. [Origen, *In epistolam ad Romanos,* bk. III, ch. viii.]

[44] [Augustine, *In Psalmum lxxxv,* enarr. 17; *Enchiridion,* ch. lxvii (the marginal reference to this work was dropped from the *Defence*); *De civitate Dei,* bk. XXI, ch. xxvi (also dropped from *Defence*); *Hypomnesticon contra Pelagianos et Coelestianos,* commonly called *Libri Hypognosticon,* bk. V, ch. v. This work is falsely attributed to Augustine.]

hath there grown up such a harvest of those Massmongers, the Masses being sold abroad commonly in every corner, the temples of God became shops, to get money; and silly souls were persuaded that nothing was more necessary to be bought. Indeed there was nothing more gainful for these men to sell.

As touching the multitude of vain and superfluous ceremonies, we know that Augustine did grievously complain of them in his own time; [45] and therefore have we cut off a great number of them, because we know that men's consciences were encumbered about them and the churches of God overladen with them. Nevertheless we keep still and esteem, not only those ceremonies which we are sure were delivered us from the apostles, but some others too besides which we thought might be suffered without hurt to the church of God; because we had a desire that all things in the holy congregation might (as Paul commandeth) "be done with comeliness, and in good order"; [46] but, as for all those things which we saw were either very superstitious, or unprofitable, or noisome, or mockeries, or contrary to the Holy Scriptures, or else unseemly for sober and discreet people, whereof there be infinite numbers nowadays where the Roman religion is used, these, I say, we have utterly refused without all manner exception, because we would not have the right worshiping of God any longer defiled with such follies.

We make our prayers in that tongue which all our people, as meet is, may understand, to the end they may (as Paul counselleth us) [47] take common commodity by common prayer; even as all the holy fathers and catholic bishops, both in the Old and New Testament, did use to pray themselves and taught the people to pray too, lest, as Augustine saith, "like parrots and ousels [48] we should seem to speak that we understand not." [49]

[45] [Augustine, *Ad inquisitiones Januarii,* liber secundus, epistola LV (alias 119). Cf. ch. xix.]

[46] [I Cor. 14:40.] [47] [I Cor. 14.]

[48] [An "ousel" or "ouzel" is a blackbird.]

[49] [Augustine, *In Psalmum xviii,* enarr. 2, sec. 1.]

Neither have we any other mediator and intercessor, by whom we may have access to God the Father, than Jesus Christ, in whose only name all things are obtained at his Father's hand. But it is a shameful part, and full of infidelity, that we see everywhere used in the churches of our adversaries, not only in that they will have innumerable sorts of mediators, and that utterly without the authority of God's word; so that, as Jeremiah saith, the saints be now "as many in number, or rather above the number of the cities"; [50] and poor men cannot tell to which saint it were best to turn them first; and though there be so many as they cannot be told, yet every one of them hath his peculiar duty and office assigned unto him of these folks, what thing they ought to ask, what to give, and what to bring to pass. But besides this also, in that they do not only wickedly, but also shamelessly, call upon the Blessed Virgin, Christ's mother, to have her remember that she is a mother and to command her Son and to use a mother's authority over him.[51]

We say also that every person is born in sin and leadeth his life in sin; that nobody is able truly to say his heart is clean; that the most righteous person is but an unprofitable servant; that the law of God is perfect and requireth of us perfect and full obedience; that we are able by no means to fulfill that law in this worldly life; that there is no one mortal creature which can be justified by his own deserts in God's sight; and therefore that our only succor and refuge is to fly to the mercy of our Father by Jesus Christ and assuredly to persuade our minds that he is the obtainer of forgiveness for our sins and that by his blood all our spots of sin be washed clean; that he hath pacified and set at one all things by the blood of his cross; that he by the same one only sacrifice which he once offered upon the cross

[50] [Jer. 2:28, 11:13.]

[51] Bernardus. [This reference was deleted in the *Defence.* For another possible reference see Jewel, *Works,* III, 571, n. 25. Here Bonaventura (thirteenth-century Franciscan) and his *Corona B. Mariae Virg.* are cited.]

hath brought to effect and fulfilled all things, and that for that cause he said, when he gave up the ghost, "It is finished"; as though he would signify that the price and ransom was now full paid for the sin of all mankind. If there be any then that think this sacrifice not sufficient, let them go in God's name and seek another that is better. We, verily, because we know this to be the only sacrifice, are well content with it alone and look for none other; and, forasmuch as it was to be offered but once, we command it not to be renewed again. And because it was full and perfect in all points and parts, we do not ordain in place thereof any continual succession of offerings.

Besides, though we say we have no meed [52] at all by our own works and deeds, but appoint all the means of our salvation to be in Christ alone, yet say we not that for this cause men ought to live loosely and dissolutely; nor that it is enough for a Christian to be baptized only and to believe; as though there were nothing else required at his hand. For true faith is lively and can in no wise be idle. Thus therefore teach we the people that God hath called us, not to follow riot and wantonness, but, as Paul saith,[53] "unto good works to walk in them"; that God hath plucked us out "from the power of darkness, to serve the living God," to cut away all the remnants of sin, and "to work our salvation in fear and trembling"; that it may appear how that the Spirit of sanctification is in our bodies and that Christ himself doth dwell in our hearts.[54]

To conclude: we believe that this our selfsame flesh wherein we live, although it die and come to dust, yet at the last day it shall return again to life, by the means of Christ's Spirit which dwelleth in us; and that then verily, whatsoever we suffer here in the meanwhile for his sake, Christ will wipe from off our eyes all tears and lamentation; and that we through him shall enjoy everlasting life and shall forever be with him in glory. So be it.

[52] ["Meed" is a word which in this place means "reward."]
[53] [Eph. 2:10.] [54] [Rom. 8:11.]

# Part III

BEHOLD, these are the horrible heresies for the which a good part of the world is at this day condemned by the Bishop of Rome, and yet were never heard to plead their cause. He should have commenced his suit rather against Christ, against the apostles, and against the holy fathers. For these things did not only proceed from them, but were also appointed by them: except perhaps these men will say (as I think they will indeed) that Christ hath not instituted the Holy Communion to be divided amongst the faithful; or that Christ's apostles and the ancient fathers have said private Masses in every corner of the temples, now ten, now twenty together in one day; or that Christ and his apostles banished all the common people from the sacrament of his blood; or that the thing which themselves do at this day everywhere, and do it so as they condemn him for an heretic which doth otherwise, is not called of Gelasius, their own doctor, plain sacrilege; or that these be not the very words of Ambrose, Augustine, Gelasius, Theodoret, Chrysostom, and Origen: "The bread and wine in the sacraments remain still the same they were before"; "The thing which is seen upon the holy table is bread"; "There ceaseth not to be still the substance of bread and nature of wine"; "The substance and nature of bread are not changed"; "The selfsame bread, as touching the material substance, goeth into the belly, and is cast out into the privy";[1] or that Christ, the apostles, and holy fathers prayed not in that tongue which the people might understand; or that Christ hath not performed all things by that one offering which he once offered upon the cross; or that the same sacrifice was imperfect and so now we have need of another. All these things must they of necessity say, unless perchance they had rather say thus, that all law and right is locked up in the treasury of the Pope's breast, and that (as once one of his soothing pages and claw-backs did not stick to say) the Pope is able to dispense against the apostles, against a council, and against the canons and rules of the apostles; and that he is not bound to stand neither by the examples, nor to the ordinances, nor to the laws of Christ.[2] We, for our parts, have learned these things of Christ, of the apostles, of the devout fathers; and do sincerely and with good faith teach the people of God the same. Which thing is the only cause why we at this day are called heretics of the chief prelates (no doubt) of religion. O immortal God! hath Christ himself then, the apostles, and so many fathers, all at once gone astray? Were then Origen, Ambrose, Augustine, Chrysostom, Gelasius, Theodoret, forsakers of the catholic faith? Was so notable a consent of so many ancient bishops and learned men nothing else but a conspiracy of heretics? Or is that now condemned in us which was then commended in them? Or is the thing now, by alteration only of men's affection, suddenly become schismatic which in them was counted catholic? Or shall that which in times past was true, now by and by, because it liketh not these men, be judged false? Let them then bring forth another Gospel, and let them show the causes why these things, which so long have openly been observed and well allowed in the church of God,

[1] [See previous references in Part II (pp. 33–34).]

[2] Dist. 36. lector, in Glossa; Dist. 82. ca. Presbyter. [For notes on these references from the *Corpus juris canonici*, see Jewel, *Works*, III, 599 and 218.]

ought now in the end to be called in again. We know well enough that the same word which was opened by Christ and spread abroad by the apostles is sufficient, both to our salvation, and also to uphold and maintain all truth, and also to confound all manner of heresy. By that word only do we condemn all sorts of the old heretics, whom these men say we have called out of hell again. As for the Arians, the Eutychians, the Marcionites, the Ebionites, the Valentinians, the Carpocratians, the Tatians, the Novatians,[3] and, shortly, all them which have had a wicked opinion, either of God the Father, or of Christ, or of the Holy Ghost, or of any other point of the Christian religion, forsomuch as they be confuted by the Gospel of Christ, we plainly pronounce them for detestable and castaway persons, and defy them even unto the devil. Neither do we leave them so, but we also severely and straitly hold them in by lawful and politic punishments, if they fortune to break out anywhere and bewray themselves.

Indeed we grant that certain new and very strange sects, as the Anabaptists,[4] Libertines,[5] Menonians,[6] and Schwenkfeldians,[7] have been stirring in the world ever since the Gospel did first spring. But the world seeth now right well (thanks be given to our God), that we neither have bred, nor taught, nor kept up these monsters. In good fellowship, I pray thee, whosoever

[3] [Jewel here enumerates a list of heretics in the first five centuries of the church's history.]

[4] [Anabaptists were those on the "left wing" of the Reformation of the sixteenth century who generally insisted upon "believers'" or "adult baptism."]

[5] [Libertines were members of a sixteenth-century Flemish sect of Antinomians (those who believed that Christians are set free by grace from the observance of moral law).]

[6] [Menonians, or Mennonites, were Anabaptists who were followers of the sixteenth-century reformer, Menno Simons.]

[7] [Schwenkfeldians were followers of Caspar Schwenkfeld (d. 1561), a reformer who could not accept the Lutheran teaching on the Eucharist and was troubled by the doctrine of justification by faith alone.]

thou be, read our books: they are to be sold in every place. What hath there ever been written by any of our company which might plainly bear with the madness of any of those heretics? Nay, I say unto you, there is no country at this day so free from their pestilent infections as they be wherein the Gospel is freely and commonly taught. So that, if they weigh the very matter with earnest and upright advertisement, this thing is a great argument that this same doctrine which we teach is the very truth of the Gospel of Christ: for lightly neither is cockle wont to grow without the wheat, nor yet the chaff without the corn. For from the very apostles' times, who knoweth not how many heresies did rise up even together so soon as the Gospel was first spread abroad? Who ever had heard tell of Simon, Menander, Saturninus, Basilides, Carpocrates, Cerinthus, Ebion, Valentinus, Secundus, Marcosius, Colorbasius, Heracleon, Lucianus, and Severus [8] before the apostles were sent abroad? But why stand we reckoning up these? Epiphanius rehearseth up fourscore sundry heresies, and Augustine many more, which did spring up even together with the Gospel. What then? Was the Gospel therefore not the Gospel, because heresies sprang up withal? Or was Christ therefore not Christ?

And yet, as we said, doth not this great crop and heap of heresies grow up amongst us which do openly, abroad, and frankly teach the Gospel? These poisons take their beginnings, their increasings and strength amongst our adversaries, in blindness and in darkness, amongst whom truth is with tyranny and cruelty kept under and cannot be heard but in corners and secret meetings. But let them make a proof, let them give the Gospel free passage, let the truth of Jesus Christ give his clear light and stretch forth his bright beams into all parts, and then shall they forthwith see how all these shadows straight will vanish and pass away at the light of the Gospel, even as the thick mist of the night consumeth at the sight of the sun. For

[8] [A list of heretics in the early church.]

whilst these men sit still, and make merry, and do nothing, we continually repress and put back all those heresies which they falsely charge us to nourish and maintain.

Where they say that we have fallen into sundry sects, and would be called some of us Lutherans, some of us Zwinglians, and cannot yet well agree among ourselves touching the whole substance of our doctrine; what would these men have said if they had been in the first times of the apostles and holy fathers; when one said, "I hold of Paul"; another, "I hold of Cephas"; another "I hold of Apollo"? [9] When Paul did so sharply rebuke Peter? [10] When, upon a falling out, Barnabas departed from Paul? [11] When, as Origen mentioneth, the Christians were divided into so many factions as that they kept no more but the name of Christians in common among them, being in no manner of thing else like to Christians? When, as Socrates saith, for their dissensions and sundry sects they were laughed and jested at openly of the people in their stages and common game plays? [12] When, as Constantine the Emperor affirmeth, there were such a number of variances and brawlings in the church that it might justly seem a misery far passing all the former miseries? When also Theophilus,[13] Epiphanius,[14] Chrysostom, Augustine, Rufinus, Jerome, being all Christians, being all fathers, being all catholics, did strive one against another with most bitter and remediless contentions without end? When, as saith Nazianzene, the parts of one body were consumed and wasted one of another? When the whole east part of the church was divided from the west, only for leavened bread and only for keeping of Easter Day, which were indeed no great matters to be strived for? And when in all councils new creeds and new decrees continually were devised? What would these men (trow ye) have

[9] [I Cor. 1:12.] [10] [Gal. 2:11.] [11] [Acts 15:39.]

[12] [Socrates (d. 450, "Scholasticus," church historian), *Church History*, bk. I, ch. vi.]

[13] [Theophilus, Patriarch of Alexandria, 385–412.]

[14] [Epiphanius (ca. 315–403), Bishop of Salamis, monastic enthusiast, and defender of the "Nicaean faith" against heretics.]

said in those days? Which side would they specially have taken? And which would they then have forsaken? Which Gospel would they have believed? Whom would they have accounted for heretics and whom for catholics? And yet what a stir and revel keep they at this time upon two poor names only, Luther and Zwingli! Because these two men are not yet fully resolved upon some one certain point of doctrine, therefore would they needs have us think that both of them were deceived; that neither of them had the Gospel; and that neither of them taught the truth aright.

But good God! What manner of fellows be these which blame us for disagreeing? And do all they themselves, ween [15] you, agree well together? Is every one of them fully resolved what to follow? Hath there been no strifes, no debates, among them at no time? Why then do the Scotists [16] and Thomists,[17] about that they call *meritum congrui* and *meritum condigni,*[18] no better agree together? Why agree they no better among themselves concerning original sin in the Blessed Virgin; concerning a solemn vow and a single vow? Why say the canonists that auricular confession is appointed by the positive law of man; and their schoolmen contrariwise, that it is appointed by the law of God? Why doth Albert Pius [19] dissent from Cajetan? [20]

[15] [I.e., believe.]

[16] [Name for the followers of John Duns Scotus (ca. 1264–1308), scholastic philosopher who gave primacy to love and will as opposed to the Thomist emphasis on knowledge and reason.]

[17] [Name for the followers of Thomas Aquinas (ca. 1225–1274), philosopher and theologian.]

[18] [The doctrine of merit was concerned with man's earning God's reward for works done. "Condign merit confers a claim to reward due in justice to services rendered, whilst congruous merit may only claim the reward on grounds of fitness" (*Oxford Dictionary of the Christian Church,* ed. F. L. Cross [Oxford, 1957], p. 888).]

[19] [In the Latin original it is indicated that Albert Pighi (Pighius) is meant here. This theologian of the Roman Church defended tradition as a source of Christian truth equal to Scripture.]

[20] [Thomas de Vio Cajetan (1469–1534), Roman Catholic theologian, general of the Dominican Order, opponent of Martin Luther, and writer of commentaries on the Bible.]

Why doth Thomas dissent from Lombard,[21] Scotus from Thomas, Occam[22] from Scotus, Alliaco[23] from Occam? And why do their Nominals disagree from their Reals?[24] And yet say I nothing of so many diversities of friars and monks; how some of them put a great holiness in eating of fish, and some in eating of herbs; some in wearing of shoes, and some in wearing of sandals; some in going in a linen garment, and some in woolen; some of them called white, some black; some being shaven broad, and some narrow; some stalking abroad upon pattens, some barefooted; some girt, and some ungirt. They ought, I wis, to remember how there be some of their own company which say that the body of Christ is in his supper naturally; contrary, other some of the selfsame company deny it to be so: again, that there be other of them which say the body of Christ in the Holy Communion is rent and torn with teeth; and some again that deny the same.[25] Some also of them there be which write that the body of Christ in the sacrament is *quantum in Eucharistia,* that is to say, has his perfect quantity in the sacrament; some other again say nay, that there be others of them which say Christ did consecrate with a certain divine power; some, that he did the same with his blessing; some again that say he did it with uttering five solemn chosen words; and some, with rehearsing the same words afterward again.[26] Some will have it that when Christ did speak those five words, the

[21] [Peter Lombard (ca. 1100–1160), "Master of the Sentences," whose textbook of Catholic theology was superseded by the works of Thomas Aquinas.]

[22] [William of Occam (ca. 1300–1349), nominalist philosopher, English Franciscan.]

[23] [Here Jewel has reference to Pierre D'Ailly (Petrus de Alliaco), who is generally known to have been greatly influenced by Occam. He lived between 1350 and 1420. Cf. Jewel, *Works,* I, 381; IV, 1105.]

[24] [I.e., nominalists versus realists.]

[25] [Stephen Gardiner (ca. 1490–1555), Bishop of Winchester,] in Diabolica Sophistica. Richardus Smith [1500–1563, Regius Professor at Oxford and later Chancellor of the University of Douai]. De consecra. recant. Bering. Schola et Glose. Cui mundus.

[26] Thomas Aquinas.

material wheaten bread was pointed unto by this demonstrative pronoun *hoc:* some had rather have that a certain *vagum individuum,* as they term it, was meant thereby.[27] Again, others there be that say dogs and mice may truly and in very deed eat the body of Christ; and others again there be that steadfastly deny it.[28] There be others which say that the very accidents of bread and wine may nourish; others again there be which say how that the substance of the bread returneth again by a miracle. What need I say more? It were overlong and tedious to reckon up all things, so very uncertain and full of doubts is yet the whole form of these men's religion and doctrine, even amongst themselves, from whence it did first spring and begin. For hardly at any time do they well agree between themselves, except it be peradventure as, in times past, the Pharisees and Sadducees, or as Herod and Pilate did accord against Christ.

They were best therefore to go and set peace at home rather among their own selves. Of a truth, unity and concord doth best become religion; yet is not unity the sure and certain mark whereby to know the church of God. For there was the greatest unity that might be amongst them that worshiped the golden calf, and amongst them which with one voice jointly cried against our Saviour Jesus Christ, "Crucify him." Neither, because the Corinthians were unquieted with private dissensions, or because Paul did square [29] with Peter or Barnabas with Paul, or because the Christians, upon the very beginning of the Gospel, were at mutual discord touching some one matter, may we therefore think there was no church of God amongst them.

[27] Stephanus Gardiner. ["Hoc est corpus meum," this is my body; "vagum individuum," undefined individual, or particle, or thing. That is, *hoc* designates something indefinable. Cf. Thomas Cranmer, *Works,* ed. J. E. Cox (Cambridge: Parker Society, 1844–1846), I, 105–106; Jewel, *Works,* II, 787–790.]

[28] De Conse. Dist. Spe. Glosa.; Magist. Sent. et Schola. [Cf. *Corpus juris canonici,* Decret. Grat., Decr. Tert. Pars, De Consecr., Dist. ii, note on canon 28, col. 1924; Jewel, *Works,* II, 782–786.]

[29] [I.e., quarrel.]

And as for those persons whom they upon spite call Zwinglians and Lutherans, in very deed they of both sides be Christians, good friends, and brethren. They vary not betwixt themselves upon the principles and foundations of our religion, nor as touching God, nor Christ, nor the Holy Ghost, nor of the means of justification, nor yet everlasting life, but upon one only question which is neither weighty nor great; [30] neither mistrust we, or make doubt at all, but they will shortly be agreed. And if there be any of them which have other opinion than is meet, we doubt not but, or [31] it be long, they will put apart all affection and names of parties, and that God will reveal the truth unto them; so that by better considering and searching out of the matter, as once it came to pass in the Council of Chalcedon, all causes and seeds of dissension shall be thoroughly plucked up by the root and be buried and quite forgotten forever; which God grant.

This is the heaviest and most grievous part of their slanders, that they call us wicked and ungodly men and say we have thrown away all care of religion. Though this ought not to trouble us much whiles they themselves that thus have charged us know full well how spiteful and untrue their slander is: for Justin the martyr is a witness, how that all Christians were called ἄθεοι that is, godless, as soon as the Gospel first began to be published and the name of Christ to be openly declared.[32] And, when Polycarp stood to be judged, the people stirred up the president to slay and murder all them which professed the Gospel, with these words, Αἶρε τοὺς ἀθέους, that is to say, "Rid out of the way these wicked and godless creatures." [33] And this was not because it was true that the Christians were godless, but

[30] [The mode of Christ's presence in the Eucharist.]

[31] [I.e., ere.]

[32] [Justin Martyr (ca. 100–165), early Christian apologist), *First Apology*, ch. vi.]

[33] Eusebius, *Church History*, bk. IV, ch. xv.]

because they would not worship stones and stocks, which were then honored as God. The whole world seeth plainly enough already what we and ours have endured at these men's hands for religion and our only God's cause. They have thrown us into prison, into water, into fire, and have imbrued themselves in our blood, not because we were either adulterers, or robbers, or murderers, but only for that we confessed the Gospel of Jesus Christ and put our confidence in the living God; and for that we complained too justly and truly (Lord, thou knowest) that they did break the law of God for their own most vain traditions; and that our adversaries were the very foes to the Gospel and enemies to Christ's cross who so wittingly and willingly did obstinately despise God's commandments.

Wherefore, when these men saw they could not rightly find fault with our doctrine, they would needs pick a quarrel and inveigh and rail against our manners, surmising how that we do condemn all well-doings; how we set open the door to all licentiousness and lust and lead away the people from all love of virtue. And in very deed, the life of all men, even of the devoutest and most Christian, both is, and evermore has been, such as one may always find some lack, even in the very best and purest conversation. And such is the inclination of all creatures unto evil, and the readiness of all men to suspect, that the things which neither have been done nor once meant to be done yet may be easily both heard and credited for true. And like as a small spot is soon spied in the neatest and whitest garment, even so the least stain of dishonesty is easily found out in the purest and sincerest life. Neither take we all them which have at this day embraced the doctrine of the Gospel to be angels and to live clearly without any mote or wrinkle; nor yet think we these men either so blind that, if anything may be noted in us, they are not able to perceive the same even through the least crevice; nor so friendly that they will construe ought to the best, nor yet so honest of nature nor courteous that they will look back upon themselves and weigh our lives by their own. If so be we list to search this matter from the bottom, we know in the very apostles' times there were Christians through whom the name of the Lord was blasphemed and evil spoken of among the gentiles. Constantius the Emperor bewaileth, as it is written in Sozomen, how that many waxed worse after they had fallen to the religion of Christ. And Cyprian in a lamentable oration setteth out the corrupt manners in his time: "The wholesome discipline," saith he, "which the apostles left unto us, hath idleness and long rest now utterly marred: everyone studied to increase his livelihood; and, clean forgetting either what they had done before whiles they were under the apostles or what they ought continually to do, having received the faith, they earnestly labored to make great their own wealth with an unsatiable desire of covetousness. There is no devout religion," saith he, "in priests, no sound faith in ministers, no charity shown in good works, no form of godliness in their conditions: men are become effeminate and women's beauty is counterfeited." [34] And before his days said Tertullian: "O, how wretched be we, which are called Christians at this time! For we live as heathens under the name of Christ." [35] And, without reciting of many more writers, Gregory Nazianzene speaketh this of the pitiful state of his own time: "We," saith he, "are in hatred among the heathen for our own vices' sake; we are also become now a wonder, not alone to angels and men, but even to all the ungodly." [36] In this case was the church of God when the Gospel first began to shine, and when the fury of tyrants was not as yet cooled, nor the sword taken off from the Christians' necks. Surely it is no new thing that men be but men, although they be called by the name of Christians.

[34] Cyprian. de Lapsis.
[35] [This citation from Tertullian is omitted in the *Defence*.]
[36] [Gregory of Nazianzus, *Oratio II, Apologetica,* secs. 83–84.]

# Part IV

BUT will these men, I pray you, think nothing at all of themselves, whiles they accuse us so maliciously and whiles they have leisure to behold so far off and see both what is done in Germany and in England? Have they either forgotten, or can they not see what is done at Rome? Or be they our accusers whose life is such as no man is able to make mention thereof but with shame and uncomeliness? Our purpose here is not to take in hand, at this present, to bring to light and open to the world those things which were meet rather to be hid and buried with the workers of them: it beseemeth neither our religion, nor our modesty, nor our shamefacedness. But yet he which giveth commandment that he should be called the vicar of Christ and the head of the church, who also heareth that such things be done in Rome, who seeth them, who suffereth them (for we will go no further), he can easily consider with himself what manner of things they be. Let him in God's name call to mind, let him remember, that they be of his own canonists which have taught the people that fornication between single folk is not sin;[1] as though they had fet[2] that doctrine from

[1] Johan de magist. de Temperantia. [Jewel here meant Martinus Magistris, *De temperantia*. He made his citation from Alphonsus de Castro, *Adversus omnes haereses* (Paris, 1543), bk. IV. Cf. Jewel, *Works,* IV, 635–636.]
[2] [I.e., fetched.]

Micio in Terence, whose words be: "It is no sin (believe me) for a young man to haunt harlots."[3] Let him remember they be of his own which have decreed that a priest ought not to be put out of his cure for fornication.[4] Let him remember also how Cardinal Campeggio,[5] Albert Pighi, and others many more of his own have taught that the priest which keepeth a concubine does live more holily and chastely than he which has a wife in matrimony. I trust he hath not yet forgotten that there be many thousands of common harlots in Rome, and that himself doth gather yearly of the same harlots about thirty thousand ducats by the way of an annual pension. Neither can he forget how himself doth maintain openly brothel houses, and by a most filthy lucre doth filthily and lewdly serve his own lust. Were all things then pure and holy in Rome when Joan, a woman rather of perfect age than of perfect life, was Pope there and bare herself as the head of the church? And after that for two whole years in that Holy See she had played the naughty pack, at last going in procession about the city, in the sight of all the cardinals and bishops, fell in travail openly in the streets?[6]

But what need one rehearse concubines and bawds as for that is now an ordinary and gainful sin at Rome? For harlots sit there nowadays, not as they did in times past, without the city walls and with their faces hid and covered,[7] but they dwell in palaces and fair houses;[8] they stray about in court and market, and that with bare and open face, as who say they

[3] [Cf. Terence, *Adelphi,* act I, sc. 2, 21–22.]

[4] 3.4.7. lata. Extra de bigimis. Quia circa. [*Corpus juris canonici,* Decret. Gratian., Decr. Sec. Pars, Causa II, Quaest. vii, note on canon 44. For "lata" read "lator." Cf. Jewel *Works,* IV, 636 ff.]

[5] [Lorenzo Cardinal Campeggio (1472–1539), canonist, diplomat, reformer.]

[6] The image of this woman Pope, being in travail, is yet to be seen at Rome. [For the discussion between Harding and Jewel concerning "Pope Joan," cf. Jewel, *Works,* IV, 648–656.]

[7] [Gen. 38:14–15.]

[8] In concilio delect. Card. Tomo. 3. [Cf. Crabbe, *Concilia,* III, col. 823.]

may not only lawfully do it but ought also to be praised for so doing. What should we say any more of this? Their vicious and abominable life is now thoroughly known to the whole world. Bernard writeth roundly and truly of the Bishop of Rome's house, yea, and of the Bishop of Rome himself. "Thy palace," saith he, "taketh in good men, but it maketh none: naughty persons thrive there and the good appair [9] and decay." [10] And whosoever he were which wrote the Tripartite work annexed to the Council *Lateranense* saith thus: "So excessive at this day is the riot, as well in the prelates and bishops as in the clerks and priests, that it is horrible to be told." [11] But these things be not only grown in ure,[12] and so by custom and continual time well allowed as all the rest of their doings in manner be, but they are now waxen old and rotten ripe. For who hath not heard what a heinous act Peter Aloysius, Pope Paul the Third's son, committed against Cosmus Cherius, the Bishop of Favense; what John Casus, Archbishop of Beneventanus, the Pope's legate at Venice, wrote in the commendation of a most abominable filthiness; and how he set forth with most loathsome words and wicked eloquence the matter which ought not once to proceed out of anybody's mouth? To whose ears hath it not come that Alphonsus Diasius, a Spaniard, being purposely sent from Rome into Germany, did shamefully and devilishly murder his own brother John Diasius, a most innocent and a most godly man, only because he had embraced the Gospel of Jesus Christ and would not return again to Rome? [13]

But it may chance to this they will say: These things may

[9] [I.e., degenerate.]

[10] [Bernard of Clairvaux (1000–1053, Cistercian monk, preacher, theologian), *De consideratione ad Eugenium Tertium,* bk. IV, ch. iv, 11.]

[11] [Cf. Crabbe, *Concilia,* Opusc. Tripart., bk. III, ch. vii, II, 1002, fourth Lateran Council.]

[12] [I.e., habit or practice.]

[13] [Jewel's authority for much of this is Johannes Sleidanus (1506–1556, annalist of the German reformation), *Commentariorum de statu religionis et reipublicae Carolo V, Caesare* (Strasbourg, 1555). For Diasius see bk. XVII. Cf. Jewel, *Works,* IV, 658 ff.]

sometime happen in the best-governed commonwealth, yea, and against the magistrates' wills; and besides, there be good laws made to punish such. I grant it be so; but by what good laws (I would know) have these great mischiefs been punished amongst them? Petrus Aloysius, after he had done that notorious act that I spake of, was always cherished in his father's bosom, Pope Paul the Third, and made his very dearling.[14] Diasius, after he had murdered his own brother, was delivered by the Pope's means, to the end he might not be punished by good laws. John Casus, *archiepiscopus Beneventanus,* is yet alive, yea, and liveth at Rome, even in the eyes and sight of the most Holy Father.

They have put to death infinite numbers of our brethren only because they believed truly and sincerely in Jesus Christ. But of that great and foul number of harlots, fornicators, adulterers, what one have they at any time (I say not killed, but) either excommunicate, or once attached?[15] Why, voluptuousness, adultery, ribaldry, whoredom, murdering of kin, incest, and other more abominable parts, are not these counted sin at Rome? Or, if they be sin, ought Christ's vicar, Peter's successor, the most Holy Father, so lightly and slyly bear them, as though they were no sin, and that in the city of Rome, and in that principal tower of all holiness?

O holy scribes and Pharisees, which knew not this kind of holiness! O what holiness, what a catholic faith is this! Peter did not thus teach at Rome; Paul did not so live at Rome; they did not practice brothelry, which these do openly; they made not a yearly revenue and profit of harlots; they suffered no common adulterers and wicked murderers to go unpunished. They did not receive them into their familiarity, into their council, into their household, nor yet into the company of Christian men. These men ought not therefore so unreasonably to triumph against our living. It had been more wisdom for them either first

[14] [I.e., darling.] [15] [I.e., arrested.]

to have proved good their own life before the world, or at least to have cloaked it a little more cunningly. For we do use still the old and ancient laws, and (as much as men may do in the manners used at these days, when all things are so wholly corrupt) we diligently and earnestly put in execution the ecclesiastical discipline; we have not common brothel houses of strumpets, nor yet flocks of concubines, nor herds of harlot haunters. Neither do we prefer adultery before matrimony; neither do we exercise beastly sensuality. Neither do we gather ordinary rents and stipends of stews, nor do suffer to escape unpunished incest and abominable naughtiness, nor yet such man-quellers as the Aloysians, Casians, and Diasians were. For, if these things would have pleased us, we needed not to have departed from these men's fellowship, amongst whom such enormities be in their chief pride and price. Neither needed we, for leaving them, to run into the hatred of men and into most willful dangers. Paul the Fourth, not many months since, had at Rome in prison certain Augustine friars, many bishops, and a great number of other devout men, for religion sake. He racked them and tormented them: to make them confess, he left no means unassayed. But in the end how many brothels, how many whoremongers, how many adulterers, how many incestuous persons could he find of all those? Our God be thanked, although we be not the men we ought and profess to be, yet, whosoever we be, compare us with these men, and even our own life and innocency will soon prove untrue and condemn their malicious surmises. For we exhort the people to all virtue and well-doing, not only by books and preachings, but also with our examples and behavior. We also teach that the Gospel is not a boasting or bragging of knowledge, but that it is the law of life, and that a Christian man (as Tertullian saith) "ought not to speak honorably, but ought to live honorably; nor that they be the hearers of the law, but the doers of the law, which are justified before God." [16]

[16] [Tertullian, *Apology*, ch. xlv.]

Besides all these matters wherewith they charge us, they are wont also to add this one thing, which they enlarge with all kind of spitefulness; that is, that we be men of trouble; that we pluck the sword and scepter out of kings' hands; that we arm the people; that we overthrow judgment places, destroy the laws, make havoc of possessions, seek to make the people princes, turn all things upside down; and, to be short, that we would have nothing in good frame in a commonwealth. Good Lord! how often have they set on fire princes' hearts with these words, to the end they might quench the light of the Gospel in the very first appearing of it, and that men might begin to hate the same or ever they were able to know it, and to the end that every magistrate might think he saw his deadly enemy as often as he saw any of us! [17]

Surely it should exceedingly grieve us to be so maliciously accused of most heinous treason, unless we knew that Christ himself, the apostles, and a number of good and Christian men were in time past blamed and reviled in like sort. For, although Christ taught they should give unto Caesar that which was Caesar's; yet was he charged with sedition in that he was accused to devise some conspiracy and to seek ways to get the kingdom. And hereupon they cried out with open mouth against him in the place of judgment, saying: "If thou let this man escape, thou art not Caesar's friend."

And though the apostles did likewise evermore and steadfastly teach that magistrates ought to be obeyed, that every soul ought to be subject to the higher powers, not only for fear of wrath and punishment but even for conscience sake, yet bare they the name to disquiet the people and to stir up the multitude to rebel. After this sort did Haman specially bring the nation of the Jews into the hatred of the King Ahasuerus, because, said he, they were a rebellious and stubborn people and

[17] [*Ibid.*, chs. i–iii.]

despised the ordinance and commandments of princes.[18] Wicked King Ahab said to Elijah, the prophet of God: "It is thou that troublest Israel."[19] Amaziah, the priest at Bethel, laid a conspiracy to the prophet Amos' charge before King Jeroboam, saying: "See, Amos hath made a conspiracy against thee in the midst of the house of Israel."[20] To be brief, Tertullian saith this was the general accusation of all Christians whiles he lived, that they were traitors, they were rebels, and the enemies of mankind.[21] Wherefore, if nowadays the truth be likewise evil spoken of, and, being the same truth it was then, if it be now like despitefully used as it was in times past, though it be a grievous and unkind dealing, yet can it not seem unto us a new or unwonted matter. Forty years ago and upward was it an easy thing for them to devise against us these accursed speeches and other sorer than these, when in the midst of the darkness of that age first began to spring and to give shine some one glimmering beam of truth unknown at that time and unheard of. When also Martin Luther and Huldreich Zwingli, being most excellent men, even sent of God to give light to the whole world, first came unto the knowledge and preaching of the Gospel; whereas yet the thing was but new and the success thereof uncertain; and when men's minds stood doubtful and amazed and their ears open to all slanderous tales; and when there could be imagined against us no fact so detestable but the people then would soon believe it for the novelty and strangeness of the matter. For so did Symmachus, so did Celsus, so did Julian, so did Porphyry,[22] the old foes of the Gospel, attempt in

[18] In the book of Hester. [Esther 3:8.] [19] [I Kings 18:17.]
[20] [Amos 7:10.] [21] [Tertullian, *Apology*, ch. xxxvii.]
[22] [Symmachus (late second-century Ebionite), Celsus (second-century pagan philosopher against whom Origen wrote), Julian (either the fourth-century emperor Julian the Apostate or the Pelagian bishop of the fourth and fifth centuries), Porphyry (the third-century Neoplatonist philosopher).]

times past to accuse all Christians of sedition and treason, before that either prince or people were able to know how those Christians were, what they professed, what they believed, or what was their meaning.

But now, sithence our very enemies do see and cannot deny but we ever in all our words and writings have diligently put the people in mind of their duty to obey their princes and magistrates, yea, though they be wicked (for this doth very trial and experience sufficiently teach, and all men's eyes, whosoever and wheresoever they be, do well enough see and witness for us), it was a foul part of them to charge us with these things; and, seeing they could find no new and late faults, therefore to seek to procure us envy only with stale and outworn lies. We give our Lord God thanks, whose only cause this is, there hath yet at no time been any such example in all the realms, dominions, and commonweals which have received the Gospel. For we have overthrown no kingdom, we have decayed no man's power or right, we have disordered no commonwealth. There continue in their own accustomed state and ancient dignity the kings of our country of England, the kings of Denmark, the kings of Sweden, the dukes of Saxony, the counties palatine, the marquesses of Brandenburg, the landgraves of Hessia, the commonwealths of the Helvetians and Rhaetians, and the free cities, as Argentine, Basle, Frankfort, Ulm, August,[23] and Nuremberg, do all, I say, abide in the same authority and estate wherein they have been heretofore, or rather in a much better for that by means of the Gospel they have their people more obedient unto them. Let them go, I pray you, into those places where at this present, through God's goodness, the Gospel is taught. Where is there more majesty? Where is there less arrogancy and tyranny? Where is the prince more honored? Where be the people less unruly? Where hath there at any time the commonwealth or the church been in more quiet?

[23] [Argentine is Strasbourg, and August is Augsburg.]

Perhaps ye will say, from the first beginning of this doctrine the common sort everywhere began to rage and to rise throughout Germany. Allow it were so, yet Martin Luther, the publisher and setter forward of this doctrine, did write marvelous vehemently and sharply against them and reclaimed them home to peace and obedience.

But, whereas it is wont sometime to be objected by persons wanting skill touching the Helvetians' change of state, and killing of Leopold the Duke of Austria, and restoring by force their country to liberty, all that was done, as appears plainly by all stories for two hundred and threescore years past or above, under Boniface the Eighth, when the authority of the Bishop of Rome was in greatest jollity, about two hundred years before Huldreich Zwingli either began to teach the Gospel or yet was born. And ever since that time they have had all things still and quiet, not only from foreign enemies, but also from civil dissension. And if it were a sin in the Helvetians to deliver their own country from foreign government, specially when they were so proudly and tyrannously oppressed, yet to burden us with other men's faults, or them with the faults of their forefathers, is against all right and reason.

But, O immortal God, and will the Bishop of Rome accuse us of treason? Will he teach the people to obey and follow their magistrates? Or hath he any regard at all of the majesty of princes? Why doth he then, as none of the old bishops of Rome heretofore ever did, suffer himself to be called of his flatterers Lord of lords,[24] as though he would have all kings and princes, who and whatsoever they are, to be his underlings? Why doth he vaunt himself to be King of kings, and to have kingly royalty over his subjects?[25] Why compelleth he all emperors and

[24] August. Steuchus. [Cf. Augustinus Steuchus (Italian theologian, d. 1549), *Opera* (Venice, 1591), De Fals, Donat. Constant; bk. I, tom. III, fol. 213, 2.]

[25] Antonius de Rosellis. [Anton de Rosellis (fl. 1450), *Monarchia*, pars prima, ch. xvii.]

princes to swear to him fealty and true obedience? Why doth he boast that the Emperor's majesty is a thousandfold inferior to him; and for this reason specially, because God has made two lights in the heaven,[26] and because heaven and earth were created not in two beginnings but in one? [27] Why hath he and his fellows (like Anabaptists and Libertines, to the end they might run on more licentiously and carelessly) shaken off the yoke and exempted themselves from being under all civil power? Why hath he his legates (as much to say as most subtle spies) lying in wait in all kings' courts, councils, and privy chambers? Why doth he, when he wishes, set Christian princes one against another and at his own pleasure trouble the whole world with debate and discord? Why doth he excommunicate and command to be taken as a heathen and a pagan any Christian prince that renounceth his authority? And why promiseth he his indulgences and his pardons so largely to any that will (what way soever it be) kill any of his enemies? Doth he maintain empires and kingdoms? or doth he once desire that common quiet should be provided for? You must pardon us, good reader, though we seem to utter these things more bitterly and bitingly than it becometh divines to do. For both the shamefulness of the matter, and the desire of rule in the Bishop of Rome, is so exceeding and outrageous that it could not well be uttered with other words, or more mildly. For he is not ashamed to say in open assembly that all jurisdiction of all kings doth depend upon himself.[28] And to feed his ambition and greediness of rule hath he pulled in pieces the empire of Rome and vexed and rent whole Christendom asunder. Falsely and traitorously also

[26] De Major et obedi. Solite. [Cf. Innocent III in *Corpus juris canonici,* Decret. Gregor. IX, bk. I, tit. xxxiii, ch. vii, col. 426.]

[27] De major. et Obedien. Unam Sanctam. [Cf. Boniface VIII in *Corpus juris canonici,* Extrav. Comm; bk. I, De Major. et Obed., ch. i, col. 212; Jewel, *Works,* I, 15, and IV, 672.]

[28] Clement V. in Concilio Vienneasi. [Cf. *Corpus juris canonici,* Clementin., bk. II, tit. ix, cap. unic. xi, ch. ii.]

did he release the Romans, the Italians, and himself too, of the oath whereby they and he were straitly bound to be true to the Emperor of Greece, and stirred up the Emperor's subjects to forsake him; and, calling Charles Martel out of France into Italy, made him Emperor, such a thing as never was seen before.[29] He put Chilperic, the French king, being no evil prince, beside his realm only because he fancied him not, and wrongfully placed Pipin in his room.[30] Again, after he had cast out King Philip, if he could have brought it so to pass, he had determined and appointed the kingdom of France to Albert, King of Romans.[31] He utterly destroyed the state of the most flourishing city and commonwealth of Florence, his own native country, and brought it out of a free and peaceable state to be governed at the pleasure of one man.[32] He brought to pass by his procurement that whole Savoy on the one side was miserably spoiled by the Emperor Charles the Fifth and on the other side by the French king, so as the unfortunate Duke had scant one city left him to hide his head in.[33]

We are cloyed with examples in this behalf, and it should be very tedious to reckon up all the notorious deeds of the bishops of Rome. Of which side were they, I beseech you, which poisoned Henry the Emperor even in the receiving of the sacrament? [34] which poisoned Victor the Pope even in the

[29] [Leo Papa III (d. 816) crowned Charlemagne Holy Roman Emperor on Christmas Day 800. Charlemagne is meant here. The error was corrected in the *Defence*.]

[30] Zacharias Papa. [Pope Zacharias (d. 752). Jewel meant Childeric III, whom this Pope confirmed in his deposition. Pipin then took the Frankish kingdom with the Pope's blessing.]

[31] [Pope Boniface VIII (ca. 1234–1303) is the one indicated here. It was he who was involved in a long struggle with Philip the Fair of France.]

[32] Clemens Papa. 7. [Clement VII, Pope from 1523 to 1534.]

[33] [*Ibid.*]

[34] [The reference here is to the supposed poisoning of Henry of Luxemburg by a Dominican monk in the year 1313. Cf. Jewel, *Works,* IV, 686–687.]

receiving of the chalice? [35] which poisoned our King John, King of England, in a drinking cup? [36] Whosoever at least they were, and of what sect soever, I am sure they were neither Lutherans nor Zwinglians. What is he at this day which alloweth the mightiest kings and monarchs of the world to kiss his blessed feet? What is he that commandeth the Emperor to go by him at his horse bridle and the French king to hold his stirrup? Who hurled under his table Francis Dandalus, the Duke of Venice, King of Crete and Cyprus, fast bound with chains, to feed of bones among his dogs? [37] Who set the imperial crown upon the Emperor Henry the Sixth his head, not with his hand but with his foot; and with the same foot again cast the same crown off, saying withal, he had power to make emperors and to unmake them again at his pleasure? [38] Who put in arms Henry the son against the Emperor his father, Henry the Fourth, and wrought so that the father was taken prisoner of his own son and, being shorn and shamefully handled, was thrust into a monastery, where with hunger and sorrow he pined away to death? [39] Who so ill-favoredly and monstrously put the Emperor Frederic's neck under his feet, and, as though that were not sufficient, added further this text out of the Psalms: "Thou shalt go upon the adder and cockatrice, and shalt tread the lion and dragon under thy feet?" [40] Such an example of scorning and condemning a prince's majesty as never before that time was heard tell of in any remembrance, except, I ween, either of Tamerlane, the King of Scythia, a wild and barbarous creature, or

[35] [Cf. J. Ranisius Textor, *Officina* (Paris, 1532), f. 27.]

[36] [Cf. Matthew Paris (ca. 1199–1259, medieval chronicler), *Historia majora,* under A.D. 1212.]

[37] Sabellicus. [Marc Antonio Sabellicus (d. 1506, Italian historian), *Rerum Venetarum ab urbe condita decades tres, & quartae libri tres,* decadis II, bk. I, col. 1220.]

[38] [Celestine III, Pope from 1191 to 1198.]

[39] [Hildebrand, Gregory VII, Bishop of Rome from 1073 to 1085.]

[40] Innocenti III. [Jewel means Alexander III (d. 1181), whose enemy was the Emperor Frederick I (Barbarossa).]

else of Sapor, King of the Persians. All these notwithstanding were Popes, all Peter's successors, all most Holy Fathers, whose several words we must take to be as good as several Gospels.

If we be counted traitors which do honor our princes, which give them all obedience, as much as is due to them by God's word, and which do pray for them, what kind of men then be these which have not only done all the things before said but also allow the same for specially well done? Do they then either this way instruct the people, as we do, to reverence their magistrate? Or can they with honesty appeach us as seditious persons, breakers of the common quiet, and despisers of princes' majesty? Truly we neither put off the yoke of obedience from us, neither do we disorder realms, neither do we set up or pull down kings, nor translate governments, nor give our kings poison to drink, nor yet hold to them our feet to be kissed, nor, opprobriously triumphing over them, leap into their necks with our feet. This rather is our profession, this is our doctrine, that every soul, of what calling soever he be, be he monk, be he preacher, be he prophet, be he apostle, ought to be subject to kings and magistrates; [41] yea, and that the Bishop of Rome himself, unless he will seem greater than the evangelists, than the prophets, or the apostles, ought both to acknowledge and to call the Emperor his lord and master, which the old Bishops of Rome, who lived in times of more grace, ever did.[42] Our common teaching also is that we ought so to obey princes as men sent of God; and that whoso withstandeth them withstandeth God's ordinance. This is our doctrine, and this is well to be seen, both in our books and in our preachings, and also in the manners and modest behavior of our people.

But, where they say we have gone away from the unity of the catholic church, this is not only a matter of malice, but be-

[41] [Chrysostom, *In epist. ad Rom.*, hom. xxiii.]

[42] Gregorius papa. saepe in epist. [Cf. Gregory the Great, *Epistolarum*, bk. V, indict. xiii, *epistola XX ad Mauricium Augustum.*]

sides, though it be most untrue, yet hath it some show and appearance of truth. For the common people and ignorant multitude give not credit alone to things true and of certainty, but even to such things also, if any chance, which may seem to have but a resemblance of truth. Therefore we see that subtle and crafty persons, when they had no truth on their side, have ever contended and hotly argued with things likely to be true, to the intent they which were not able to espy the very ground of the matter might be carried away at least with some probability or likelihood of the truth. In times past, where the first Christians, our forefathers, in making their prayers to God, did turn themselves toward the East, there were that said they worshiped the sun and reckoned it as God.[43] Again, where our forefathers said that, as touching immortal and everlasting life, they lived by no other means but by the flesh and blood of that Lamb who was without spot, that is to say, of our Saviour Jesus Christ; the envious creatures, and foes of Christ's cross, whose only care was to bring Christian religion into slander by all manner of ways, made people believe that they were wicked persons, that they sacrificed men's flesh and drunk men's blood.[44] Also, where our forefathers said that before God "there is neither man nor woman," nor, for attaining to the true righteousness, there is no distinction at all of persons, and that they did call one another indifferently by the name of sisters and brothers; there wanted not men which forged false tales upon the same, saying that the Christians made no difference among themselves, either of age or of kind, but like brute beasts without regard had to do one with another.[45] And where, for to pray and hear the Gospel, they met often together in secret and byeplaces, because rebels sometime were wont to do the like, rumors were everywhere spread abroad how they made privy confederacies and counseled together either to kill the magis-

[43] [Tertullian, *Apology,* ch. xvi.] [44] [*Ibid.,* chs. vii–ix.]
[45] [*Ibid.,* chs. iii, ix. Cf. chs. ii and viii.]

trates or to subvert the commonwealth. And where, in celebrating the holy mysteries after Christ's institution, they took bread and wine, they were thought of many not to worship Christ but Bacchus and Ceres; [46] forsomuch as those vain gods were worshiped of the heathen in like sort, after a profane superstition, with bread and wine. These things were believed of many, not because they were true indeed (for what could be more untrue?) but because they were like to be true and through a certain shadow of truth might the more easily deceive the simple.

On this fashion likewise do these men slander us as heretics and say that we have left the church and fellowship of Christ; not because they think it is true (for they do not much force of that), but because to ignorant folk it might perhaps some way appear true. We have indeed put ourselves apart, not as heretics are wont, from the church of Christ, but, as all good men ought to do, from the infection of naughty persons and hypocrites.

Nevertheless, in this point they triumph marvelously, that they be the church, that their church is Christ's spouse, the pillar of truth, the ark of Noah, and that without it there is no hope of salvation. Contrariwise they say that we be renegades, that we have torn Christ's seat, that we are plucked quite off from the body of Christ and have forsaken the catholic faith. And, when they leave nothing unspoken that may never so falsely and maliciously be said against us, yet this one thing are they never able truly to say, that we have swerved either from the word of God, or from the apostles of Christ, or from the primitive church. Surely we have ever judged the primitive church of Christ's time, of the apostles, and of the holy fathers, to be the catholic church; neither make we doubt to name it Noah's ark, Christ's spouse, the pillar and upholder of all truth, nor yet to fix therein the means of our salvation. It is doubtless

[46] [Augustine, *Contra Faustum Manichaeum,* bk. XX, ch. viii.]

an odious matter for one to leave the fellowship whereunto he has been accustomed, and specially of those men, who, though they be not, yet at least seem and be called Christians. And to say truly, we do not despise the church of these men (howsoever it be ordered by them nowadays), partly for the name sake itself, and partly for that the Gospel of Jesus Christ hath once been therein truly and purely set forth. Neither had we departed therefrom but of very necessity and much against our wills. But I put case, an idol be set up in the church of God, and the same desolation which Christ prophesied to come stood openly in the holy place.[47] What if some thief or pirate invade and possess Noah's ark? These folks, as often as they tell us of the church, mean thereby themselves alone, and attribute all these titles to their own selves, boasting as they did in times past which cried, "The temple of the Lord, the temple of the Lord"; [48] or as the Pharisees and scribes did, which cracked [49] they were "Abraham's children." [50] Thus with a gay and jolly show deceive they the simple and seek to choke us with the bare name of the church. Much like as if a thief, when he has gotten into another man's house and by violence either hath thrust out or slain the owner, should afterward assign the same house to himself, casting forth of possession the right inheritor; or if Antichrist, when he had once entered into "the temple of God," should afterward say, "This house is mine own; and Christ has nothing to do withal." For these men now, after they have left nothing remaining in the church of God that hath any likeness of this church, yet will they seem the patrons and the valiant maintainers of the church; very like as Gracchus amongst the Romans stood in defense of the treasury, notwithstanding with his prodigality and fond expenses he had utterly wasted the whole stock of the treasury. And yet was there never anything so wicked or so far out of reason but lightly it might be

[47] [Matt. 24:15.] [48] [Jer. 7:4.] [49] [I.e., boasted.]
[50] [John 8:39.]

covered and defended by the name of the church. For the wasps also make honeycombs as well as bees, and wicked men have companies like to the church of God; yet, for all that, they be not straightway the people of God which are called the people of God, neither be they all Israelites as many as are come of Israel the father.

The Arians, notwithstanding they were heretics, yet bragged they that they alone were catholics, calling all the rest, now Ambrosians, now Athanasians, now Johannites.[51] And Nestorius, as says Theodoret, for all he was an heretic, yet covered himself τῆς ὀρθοδοξίας προσχήματι,[52] that is to wit, with a certain cloak and color of the true and right faith. Ebion, though he agreed in opinion with the Samaritans, yet, as says Epiphanius, he would be called a Christian.[53] The Mahomites[54] at this day, for all that all histories make plain mention and themselves cannot deny but they took their first beginning of Hagar the bondwoman, yet, for the very name and stock's sake, choose they rather to be called Saracens, as though they came of Sara the freewoman and Abraham's wife.[55] So likewise the false prophets of all ages, which stood up against the prophets of God, which resisted Isaiah, Jeremiah, Christ, and the apostles, at no time cracked of anything so much as they did of the name of the church. And for no other cause did they so fiercely vex them and call them renegades and apostates than for that they forsook their fellowship and kept not the ordinances of the elders. Wherefore, if we would follow the judgments of those men only who then governed the church, and would respect nothing else, neither God, nor his word, it must needs

[51] [Augustine, *Epistola* 93 (alias 48), *ad Vincentio,* ch. vii, sec. 23.]

[52] [Theodoret, *Compendium haereticarum fabularum,* bk. IV, ch. xvii, *De Nestorio.*]

[53] [Epiphanius, *Adversus haereses,* bk. I, tom. II, haeres. xxx, *Adversus Ebionaeos.*]

[54] [Mohammedans.]

[55] [Sozomen, *Church History,* bk. VI, ch. xxxviii.]

be confessed that the apostles were rightly and by just law condemned of them to death because they fell from the bishops and priests, that is, you must think, from the catholic church; and because they made many new alterations in religion, contrary to the bishops' and priests' wills, yea, and for all their spurning so earnestly against it. Wherefore, like as it is written that Hercules in old time was forced, in striving with Antaeus, that huge giant, to lift him quite up from the earth that was his mother ere he could conquer him; even so must our adversaries be heaved from their mother, that is, from this vain color and shadow of the church, wherewith they so disguise and defend themselves; otherwise they cannot be brought to yield unto the word of God. And therefore saith Jeremiah the prophet, "Make not such great boast that the temple of the Lord is with you. This is but a vain confidence, for these are lies." [56] The angel also saith in the Apocalypse, "They say they be Jews, but they be the synagogue of Satan." [57] And Christ said to the Pharisees, when they vaunted themself of the kindred and blood of Abraham, "Ye are of your father the devil," [58] for you resemble not your father Abraham; as much to say, "Ye are not the men ye would so fain be called; ye beguile the people with vain titles and abuse the name of the church to the overthrowing of the church."

So that these men's part had been first to have clearly and truly proved that the Romish church is the true and right-instructed church of God; and that the same, as they do order it at this day, doth agree with the primitive church of Christ, of the apostles, and of the holy fathers, which we doubt not but was indeed the true catholic church. For our parts, if we could have judged ignorance, error, superstition, idolatry, men's inventions, and the same commonly disagreeing with the Holy Scriptures, either pleased God, or to be sufficient for the obtaining everlasting salvation; or if we could ascertain ourselves

[56] [Jer. 7:4.] [57] [Rev. 2:9.] [58] [John 8:44.]

that the word of God was written but for a time only, and afterward again ought to be abrogated and put away; or else that the sayings and commandments of God ought to be subject to man's will, that whatsoever God saith and commandeth, except the Bishop of Rome willeth and commandeth the same, it must be taken as void and unspoken; if we could have brought ourselves to believe these things, we grant there had been no cause at all why we should have left these men's company. As touching that we have now done, to depart from that church whose errors were proved and made manifest to the world, which church also had already evidently departed from God's word; and yet not to depart so much from itself as from the errors thereof; and not to do this disorderly or wickedly, but quietly and soberly—we have done nothing herein against the doctrine either of Christ or of his apostles. For neither is the church of God such as it may not be dusked with some spot or asketh not sometime reparation. Else what needeth there so many assemblies and councils, without the which, as saith Egidius, the Christian faith is not able to stand? "For look," saith he, "how often councils are discontinued, so often is the church destitute of Christ."[59] Or if there be no peril that harm may come to the church, what need is there to retain to no purpose the names of bishops, as is now commonly used among them? For if there be no sheep that may stray, why be they called shepherds? If there be no city that may be betrayed, why be they called watchmen? If there be nothing that may run to ruin, why be they called pillars? Anon after the first creation of the world, the church of God began to spread abroad, and the same was instructed with the heavenly word which God himself pronounced with his own mouth. It was also furnished with divine ceremonies. It was taught by the Spirit of God, by the

[59] In Concil. Lateranense sub Julio 2. [Cf. Crabbe, *Concilia,* III, 524, Aegid. Viterb. Orat. Synod. Later. Egidius is Giles of Rome (Aegidius Romanos), the medieval philosopher who died in 1316.]

patriarchs and prophets, and continued so even till the time that Christ showed himself to us in the flesh. This notwithstanding, how often, O good God, in the meanwhile, and how horribly was the same church darkened and decayed! Where was that church then when "all flesh upon earth had defiled their own way"? [60] Where was it when amongst the number of the whole world there were only eight persons (and they neither all chaste and good) whom God's will was should be saved alive from that universal destruction and mortality? When Elijah the prophet so lamentably and bitterly made moan that only himself was left of all the whole world which did truly and duly worship God? [61] And when Isaiah said, "the silver" of God's people (that is, of the church) was "become dross"; and that "the same city which aforetime had been faithful was now become an harlot"; and that in the same was "no part sound throughout the whole body, from the head to the foot?" [62] Or else, when Christ himself said that the house of God was made by the Pharisees and priests "a den of thieves"? [63] Of a truth, the church, even as a cornfield, except it be eared,[64] manured, tilled, and trimmed, instead of wheat it will bring forth thistles, darnel, and nettles. For this cause did God send, ever among, both prophets and apostles, and last of all his "own Son," who might bring home the people into the right way and repair anew the tottering church after she had erred.

But lest some man should say that the foresaid things happened in the time of the Law only, of shadows, and of infancy, when truth lay hid under figures and ceremonies, when nothing as yet was brought to perfection, when the Law was not graven in men's hearts but in stone (and yet is that but a foolish saying, for even at those days was there the very same God that is now, the same Spirit, the same Christ, the same faith, the same doctrine, the same hope, the same inheritance, the same

[60] [Gen. 6:12.] [61] [I Kings 19:10.] [62] [Isa. 1:22.]
[63] [Matt. 21:13.] [64] [I.e., plowed.]

covenant, and the same efficacy and virtue of God's word: Eusebius also saith, "All the faithful, even from Adam until Christ, were in very deed Christians,"[65] though they were not so termed; but, as I said, lest men should thus speak still), Paul the apostle found the like faults and falls even then in the prime and chief of the Gospel, in the greatest perfection, and in light, so that he was compelled to write in this sort to the Galatians, whom he had well before that instructed: "I fear me," quod he, "lest I have labored amongst you to small purpose, and lest ye have heard the Gospel in vain."[66] "O my little children, of whom I travail anew till Christ be fashioned again in you."[67] And as for the Church of the Corinthians, how foully it was defiled is nothing needful to rehearse. Now tell me, might the churches of the Galatians and Corinthians go amiss, and the Church of Rome alone may it not fail nor go amiss? Surely Christ prophesied long before of his church that the time should come when desolation should stand in the holy place.[68] And Paul saith that Antichrist should once set up his own tabernacle and stately seat in the temple of God;[69] and that the time should be "when men should not away with wholesome doctrine, but be turned back unto fables and lies," and that within the very church.[70] Peter likewise telleth how there should be teachers of lies in the church of Christ.[71] Daniel the prophet, speaking of the later times of Antichrist: "Truth," saith he, "in that season shall be thrown under foot and trodden upon in the world."[72] And Christ saith how the calamity and confusion of things shall be so exceeding great "that even the chosen, if it were possible, shall be brought into error";[73] and how all these things shall come to pass, not amongst gentiles and Turks, but that they should be in the holy place, in the

[65] Lib. 1. cap. i. [Eusebius, *Church History*, bk. I, ch. iv.]
[66] [Gal. 4:11.] [67] [Gal. 5:19.] [68] [Matt. 24:15.]
[69] [II Thess. 2:4.] [70] [II Tim. 4:3–4.] [71] [II Pet. 2:1.]
[72] [Dan. 8:12.] [73] [Matt. 24:24.]

temple of God, in the church, and in the company and fellowship of those which profess the name of Christ.

Albeit these same warnings alone may suffice a wise man to take heed he do not suffer himself rashly to be deceived with the name of the church, and not to stay to make further inquisition thereof by God's word; yet, besides all this, many fathers also, many learned and godly men, have often and carefully complained how all these things have chanced in their lifetime. For even in the midst of that thick mist of darkness God would yet there should be some who, though they gave not a clear and bright light, yet should they kindle, were it but some spark which men might espy, being in the darkness.

Hilary, when things as yet were almost uncorrupt and in good case too: "Ye are ill deceived," saith he, "with the love of walls: ye do ill worship the church, in that ye worship it in houses and buildings: ye do ill bring in the name of peace under roofs. Is there any doubt but Antichrist will have his seat under the same? I rather reckon hills, woods, pools, marshes, prisons, quavemires, to be places of more safety; for in these the prophets, either abiding of their accord or forced thither by violence, did prophesy by the Spirit of God." [74]

Gregory, as one which perceived and foresaw in his mind the wrack of all things, wrote thus of John, Bishop of Constantinople, who was the first of all others that commanded himself to be called by this new name, the universal bishop of whole Christ's church: "If the church," saith he, "shall depend upon one man, it will soon fall down to the ground." [75] Who is he that seeth not how this is come to pass long since? For long agone has the Bishop of Rome willed to have the whole

[74] Contra Auxentium. [Hilary of Poitiers (ca. 315–367, bishop, defender of orthodoxy against the Arians), *Contra Arianos, vel Auxentium Mediolanensem,* ch. xvii. Auxentius became the Arian Bishop of Milan in 355.]

[75] In Registro. b. 4. epist. 32 ad Mauri. [Jewel has reference here to Gregory, *Epistolarum,* bk. V, indict. xiii, epistola CC. Cf. Jewel, *Works,* IV, 731–732.]

church depend upon himself alone. Wherefore it is no marvel though it be clean fallen down long ago.

Bernard the abbot, above four hundred years past, writeth thus: "Nothing is now of sincerity and pureness among the clergy: wherefore it resteth that the man of sin should be revealed." [76] The same Bernard, in his treatise of the conversion of Paul: "It seemeth now," saith he, "that persecution hath ceased: no, no, persecution seemeth but now to begin, even from them which have chief preeminence in the church. Thy friends and neighbors, O God, have drawn near and stood up against thee: from the sole of thy foot to the crown of thy head there is no part whole. Iniquity is proceeded from the elders, the judges and deputies, which pretend to rule thy people. We cannot say now, 'Look how the people be, so is the priest.' For the people be not so ill as the priest is. Alas, alas, O Lord God, the selfsame persons be the chief in persecuting thee which seem to love the highest place and bear most rule in thy church!" [77] The same Bernard again, upon the Canticles, writeth thus: "All they are thy friends, yet are they all thy foes; all thy kinsfolk, yet are they all thy adversaries. Being Christ's servants, they serve Antichrist. Behold, in my rest my bitterness is most bitter." [78]

Roger Bacon also, a man of great fame, after he had in a vehement oration touched to the quick the woeful state of his own time: "These so many errors," saith he, "require and look for Antichrist." [79] Gerson complaineth how in his days all the substance and efficacy of sacred divinity was brought into a

[76] Sermone 33. [Bernard of Clairvaux, in *Psalmum XC, Qui Habitat,* sermo VI, sec. 7.]

[77] [Cf. Bernard, *In conversione S. Pauli,* sermo. I, sec. iii.]

[78] [Cf. Bernard, *Sermones in Cantia Canticorum,* sermo. XXIII, secs. 15–16.]

[79] In libello de idiomate linguarum. [This passage has not been located. Cf. Jewel, *Works,* IV, 735–736. Roger Bacon was a thirteenth-century Franciscan philosopher.]

glorious contention and ostentation of wits and to very sophistry.[80] The poor men called *pauperes a Lugduno,* men, as touching the manner of their life, not to be misliked, were wont boldly to affirm that the Romish church (from whence alone all counsel and orders was then sought) was the very same harlot of Babylon and rout of devils whereof is prophesied so plainly in the Apocalypse.

I know well enough the authority of the foresaid persons is but lightly regarded amongst these men. How then if I call forth those for witnesses whom themselves have used to honor? What if I say that Hadrian [81] the Bishop of Rome did frankly confess that all these mischiefs brast [82] out first from the high throne of the Pope? Pighi acknowledgeth herein to be a fault, that many abuses are brought in, even into the very Mass, which Mass otherwise he would have seem to be a reverend matter.[83] Gerson saith that through the number of most fond ceremonies all the virtue of the Holy Ghost, which ought to have full operation in us, and all true godliness, is utterly quenched and dead.[84] Whole Greece and Asia complain how the Bishops of Rome, with the marts of their purgatories and pardons, have both tormented men's consciences and picked their purses.

As touching the tyranny of the Bishops of Rome and their barbarous Persian-like pride, to leave out others, whom perchance they reckon for enemies because they freely and liberally find fault with their vices, the selfsame men which have led

[80] [Cf. Jean Gerson (1363–1469, French ecclesiastic, author), *Sermo de calam, eccles. et de sign. fut. Jud.* However, the exact words used by Jewel are not to be found there. Cf. Jewel, *Works,* IV, 736, n. 4.]

[81] Platina. [Hadrian VI, Pope from 1522 to 1523, is meant here. Cf. Sleidanus, *Commentariorum,* bk. IV, under A.D. 1523.]

[82] [I.e., burst.]

[83] [Cf. Albertus Pighius, *Explic. Cathol. controv.* (Paris, 1586), contr. VII, De Miss. Priv., f. 123(2).]

[84] [Cf. Jean Gerson, *Lib. de vit. spirit. anim.,* lect. ii.]

their life at Rome, in the holy city, in the face of the most Holy Father, who also were able to see all their secrets and at no time departed from the catholic faith, as for example, Lorenzo Valla, Marsiglio of Padua, Francesco Petrarch, Girolamo Savonarola, Abbot Joachim, Baptist of Mantua,[85] and before all these, Bernard the abbot, have many a time and much complained of it, giving the world also sometime to understand that the Bishop of Rome himself (by your leave) is very Antichrist. Whether they spake it truly or falsely, let that go: sure I am they spake it plainly. Neither can any man allege that those authors were Luther's or Zwingli's scholars, for they lived not only certain years, but also certain ages, or ever Luther's or Zwingli's names were heard of. They well saw that even in their days errors had crept into the church and wished earnestly they might be amended.

And what marvel if the church were then carried away with errors in that time, specially when neither the Bishop of Rome, who then only ruled the roost, nor almost any other, either did his duty or once understood what was his duty. For it is hard to be believed, whiles they were idle and fast asleep, that the devil also all that while either fell asleep or else continually lay idle. For how they were occupied in the meantime, and with what faithfulness they took care of God's house, though we hold our peace, yet, I pray you, let them hear Bernard, their own friend. "The bishops," saith he, "who now have charge of God's church, are not teachers, but deceivers: they are not feeders, but beguilers: they are not prelates, but Pilates." [86]

[85] [Lorenzo Valla (ca. 1406–1457), Italian humanist, biblical scholar, a founder of modern historical criticism; Marsiglio of Padua (ca. 1275–1342), author of *Defensor pacis;* Francesco Petrarch (1304–1374), early Italian humanist; Girolamo Savonarola (1452–1498), Dominican friar, reformer in Florence; Joachim of Fiore (ca. 1132–1202), Italian mystic and author of apocalyptic works; Baptista (Spagnuoli) of Mantua (1447–1516), Renaissance poet.]

[86] [Bernard, *De consideratione ad Eugenium Tertium,* bk. II, ch. viii, 15–16.]

These words spake Bernard of that bishop who named himself the highest bishop of all, and of the other bishops likewise which then had the place of government. Bernard was no Lutheran; Bernard was no heretic; he had not forsaken the catholic church; yet nevertheless he did not let to call the bishops that were then deceivers, beguilers, and Pilates. Now when the people was openly deceived, and Christian men's eyes were craftily bleared, and when Pilate sat in judgment place and condemned Christ and Christ's members to the sword and fire, O good Lord, in what case was Christ's church then? But yet tell me, of so many and gross errors, what one have these men at any time reformed, or what fault have they once acknowledged and confessed?

But, forsomuch as these men avouch the universal possession of the catholic church to be their own, and call us heretics because we agree not in judgment with them, let us know, I beseech you, what proper mark and badge hath that church of theirs whereby it may be known to be the church of God. I wis it is not so hard a matter to find out God's church, if a man will seek it earnestly and diligently. For the church of God is set upon a high and glistering place, in the top of an hill,[87] and built upon the foundation of the apostles and prophets.[88] "There," saith Augustine, "let us seek the church: there let us try our matter." [89] "And," as he saith again in another place, "the church must be showed out of the holy and canonical Scriptures; and that which cannot be showed out of them is not the church." [90] Yet, for all this, I wot not how, whether it be for fear, or for conscience, or despairing of victory, these men alway abhor and fly the word of God, even as the thief

[87] [Isa. 2:2.] [88] [Eph. 2:20.]

[89] [Cf. Augustine, *Epistola ad catholicos contra Donatistas, vulgo de unitate ecclesiae,* ch. iii, sec. 5.]

[90] [*Ibid.,* chs. iii and iv.]

fleeth the gallows. And no wonder truly. For, like as men say the *cantharus*[91] by and by perisheth and dieth as soon as it is laid in balm, notwithstanding balm be otherwise a most sweet-smelling ointment, even so these men well see their own matter is damped and destroyed in the word of God, as if it were in poison. Therefore the Holy Scriptures, which our Saviour Jesus Christ did not only use for authority in all his speech but did also at last seal up the same with his own blood, these men, to the intent they might with less business drive the people from the same, as from a thing dangerous and deadly, have used to call them a bare letter, uncertain, unprofitable, dumb, killing, and dead: which seems to us all one as if they should say, "The Scriptures are to no purpose, or as good as none." Hereunto they add also a similitude not very agreeable, how the Scriptures be like to a nose of wax or a shipman's hose; how they may be fashioned and plied all manner of ways and serve all men's turns.[92] Wotteth not the Bishop of Rome that these things are spoken by his own minions? or understandeth he not he hath such champions to fight for him? Let him hearken then how holily and how godly one Hosius[93] writeth of this matter, a bishop in Polonia, as he testifieth of himself; a man doubtless well spoken and not unlearned, and a very sharp and stout maintainer of that side. One will marvel, I suppose, how a good man could either conceive so wickedly or write so despitefully of those words which he knew proceeded from God's mouth, and specially in such sort as he would not have it seem his own private opinion alone but the common opinion of all that band. He dissembleth, I grant you indeed, and hideth what he is, and setteth forth the matter so as though it were not he and

[91] [By "cantharus" Jewel meant a kind of beetle probably of the family Cantharidae.]

[92] [Albertus Pighius, *Hierarchiae ecclesiasticae assertio* (Cologne, 1538), bk. III, ch. iii.]

[93] [Stanislaus Hosius (1504–1579), a Polish cardinal and theologian.]

his side but the Schwenkfeldian heretics that so did speak.[94] "We," saith he, "will bid away with the same Scriptures, whereof we see brought not only divers, but also contrary, interpretations; and we will hear God speak rather than we will resort to these naked elements or bare words of the Scriptures and appoint our salvation to rest in them. It behooveth not a man to be expert in the Law and Scripture, but to be taught of God. It is but lost labor that a man bestoweth in the Scriptures. For the Scripture is a creature and a certain bare letter." [95] This is Hosius' saying, uttered altogether with the same spirit and the same mind wherewith in times past the heretics Montanus and Marcion were moved, who, as it is written of them, used to say, when with a contempt they rejected the Holy Scriptures, that themselves knew many more and better things than either Christ or the apostles ever knew.

What then shall I say here, O ye principal posts of religion, O ye arch-governors of Christ's church? Is this that your reverence which ye give to God's word? The Holy Scriptures, which St. Paul saith came "by the inspiration of God," which God did commend by so many miracles, wherein are the most perfect prints of Christ's own steps, which all the holy fathers, apostles, and angels, which Christ himself the son of God, as often as was needful, did allege for testimony and proof; will ye, as though they were unworthy for you to hear, bid them avaunt away? That is, will ye enjoin God to keep silence, who speaketh to you most clearly by his own mouth in the Scriptures? Or that word, whereby alone, as Paul saith, we are reconciled to God, and which the prophet David saith is "holy and pure, and shall last forever," will ye call that but a bare

[94] [This sentence is not in the Latin edition. It first appeared in *An Apologie* (London, 1562), f. 38. On the whole treatment of this section in which Jewel is accused of misquoting Hosius, cf. Jewel, *Works*, IV, 753–761.]

[95] [S. Hosius, *De expresso Dei verbo* (Worms, 1558), sig. O. ii.]

and dead letter?[96] Or will ye say that all our labor is lost which is bestowed in that thing which Christ hath commanded us diligently to search and to have evermore before our eyes?[97] And will ye say that Christ and the apostles meant with subtlety to deceive the people when they exhorted them to read the Holy Scriptures, that thereby they might flow in all wisdom and knowledge? No marvel at all though these men despise us and all our doings, which set so little by God himself and his infallible sayings. Yet was it but want of wit in them, to the intent they might hurt us, to do so extreme injury to the word of God.

But Hosius will here make exclamation, saying we do him wrong and that these be not his own words but the words of the heretic Schwenkfeld. But how then if Schwenkfeld make exclamation on the other side and say that the same very words be not his but Hosius' own words? For tell me, where hath Schwenkfeld ever written them? Or, if he have written them, and Hosius have judged the same to be wicked, why hath not Hosius spoken so much as one word to confute them? Howsoever the matter goeth, although Hosius peradventure will not allow of those words, yet he doth not disallow the meaning of the words. For well near in all controversies, and namely, touching the use of the Holy Communion under both kinds, although the words of Christ be plain and evident, yet doth Hosius disdainfully reject them as no better than cold and dead elements, and commandeth to give faith to certain new lessons, appointed by the church, and to I wot not what revelations of the Holy Ghost. And Pighi saith: "Men ought not to believe, no not the most clear and manifest words of the Scriptures, unless the same be allowed for good by the interpretation and authority of the church."[98]

[96] [Psalm 19:8,9.] [97] [John 5:39.]

[98] [Pighius, *Hierarchiae,* bk. I, ch. ii. The entire preceding paragraph was added in the first English translation, *An Apologie* (1562), f. 38(2).]

And yet, as though this were too little, they also burn the Holy Scriptures, as in times past wicked King Aza did, or as Antiochus or Maximinus did, and are wont to name them heretics' books. And out of doubt, as it seems, they would fain do as Herod in old time did in Jewry, that he might with more surety keep still his usurped dominion; who, being an Idumaean born and a stranger to the stock and kindred of the Jews, and yet coveting much to be taken for a Jew, to the end he might establish to him and his posterity the kingdom of that country which he had gotten of Augustus Caesar, he commanded all the genealogies and pedigrees to be burnt and made out of the way, so as there should remain no record whereby he might be known to them that came after that he was an alien in blood; whereas even from Abraham's time these monuments had been safely kept amongst the Jews and laid up in their treasury, because in them it might easily and most assuredly be found of what lineage every one did descend.[99] So (in good faith) do these men, when they would have all their own doings in estimation as though they had been delivered to us even from the apostles, or from Christ himself, to the end there might be found nowhere anything able to convince such their dreams and lies, either they burn the Holy Scriptures, or else they craftily convey them from the people surely.

Very rightly and aptly doth Chrysostom write against these men. "Heretics," saith he, "shut up the doors against the truth; for they know full well if the door were open the church should be none of theirs."[100] Theophylact also: "God's word," saith he, "is the candle whereby the thief is espied."[101] And Tertullian saith: "The Holy Scripture manifestly finds out the fraud and theft of heretics."[102] For why do they hide, why do they

[99] [Eusebius, *Church History,* bk. I, ch. vii.]

[100] [Chrysostom, *Opus imperfectum in Matthaeum,* hom. xliv, ex cap. xxiii. This is a spurious writing.]

[101] [Theophylact, *Enarratio in Euangelium Lucae,* ch. xvi, on Luke 16:31.]

[102] [Tertullian, *De Trinitate.* This work is attributed to Novatian, the third-century Roman presbyter.]

keep under, the Gospel which Christ would have preached aloud from the housetop? Why whelm they that light under a bushel which ought to stand on a candlestick? Why trust they more to the blindness of the unskillful multitude, and to ignorance, than to the goodness of their cause? Think they their sleights are not already perceived, and that they can walk now unespied, as though they had Gyges' ring to go invisible by upon their finger? No, no. All men see now well and well again what good stuff is in that chest of the Bishop of Rome's bosom. This thing alone of itself may be an argument sufficient that they work not uprightly and truly. Worthily ought that matter seem suspicious which fleeth trial and is afraid of the light. "For he that doth evil," as Christ saith, "seeketh darkness and hateth light." [103] A conscience that knoweth itself clear cometh willingly into open show, that the works which proceed of God may be seen. Neither be they so very blind but they see this well enough, how their own kingdom straightway is at a point if the Scripture once have the upper hand; and that, like as men say, the idols of devils in times past, of whom men in doubtful matters were then wont to receive answers, were suddenly stricken dumb at the sight of Christ when he was born and came into the world; even so they see that now all their subtle practices will soon fall down headlong upon the sight of the Gospel. For Antichrist is not overthrown but with the brightness of Christ's coming.[104]

As for us, we run not for succor to the fire, as these men's guise is, but we run to the Scriptures; neither do we reason with sword, but with the word of God: and therewith, as saith Tertullian, "do we feed our faith; by it do we stir up our hope and strengthen our confidence." [105] For we know that the "Gospel of Jesus Christ is the power of God unto salvation"; [106] and that therein consisteth eternal life. And, as Paul warneth us, "We do not hear, no not an angel of God coming from

[103] [John 3:20.] [104] [II Thess. 2:8.]
[105] [Tertullian, *Apology*, ch. xxxix.] [106] [Rom. 1:16.]

heaven, if he go about to pull us from any part of this doctrine."[107] Yea, more than this, as the holy martyr Justin speaketh of himself, we would give no credence to God himself if he should teach us any other Gospel.[108]

For where these men bid the Holy Scriptures away as dumb and fruitless and procure us to come to God himself rather, who speaketh in the church and in councils, which is to say, to believe their fancies and opinions; this way of finding out the truth is uncertain and exceeding dangerous, and in manner a fantastical and a mad way, and by no means allowed of the holy fathers. Chrysostom saith: "There be many oftentimes which boast themselves of the Holy Ghost; but truly whoso speak of their own head do falsely boast they have the Spirit of God. For, like as (saith he) Christ denied he spake of himself when he spake out of the Law and prophets; even so now, if anything be pressed upon us in the name of the Holy Ghost save the Gospel, we ought not to believe it. For, as Christ is the fulfilling of the Law and the prophets, so is the Holy Ghost the fulfilling of the Gospel."[109] Thus far goeth Chrysostom.

[107] [Gal. 1:8.]

[108] [This sentence was later omitted, having been added in the Bacon translation. No marginal reference is given to a particular place in Justin's works.]

[109] [Chrysostom, *Sermo de Sancto Spiritu,* ch. iii. This is no longer attributed to Chrysostom.]

# Part V

BUT here I look they will say, though they have not the Scriptures, yet maychance they have the ancient doctors and holy fathers with them. For this is a high brag they have ever made, how that all antiquity and a continual consent of all ages doth make on their side; and that all our cases be but new and yesterday's work and until these few last years never heard of. Questionless, there can nothing be more spitefully spoken against the religion of God than to accuse it of novelty, as a new-come-up matter: for, as there can be no change in God himself, so ought there to be no change in his religion.

Yet nevertheless, we wot not by what means, but we have ever seen it come so to pass from the first beginning of all that as often as God did give but some light and did open his truth unto men, though the truth were not only of greatest antiquity but also from everlasting, yet of wicked men and of the adversaries was it called newfangled and of late devised. That ungracious and bloodthirsty Haman, when he sought to procure the King Ahasuerus' displeasure against the Jews, this was his accusation to him: "Thou hast here," saith he, "a kind of people that useth certain new laws of their own, but stiff-necked and rebellious against all thy laws."[1] When Paul also

[1] [Esther 3:8.]

began first to preach and expound the Gospel at Athens, he was called a tidings-bringer of new gods, as much to say as of new religion; for (said the Athenians) "may we not know of thee what new doctrine this is?"[2] Celsus likewise, when he of set purpose wrote against Christ, to the end he might more scornfully scoff out the Gospel by the name of novelty: "What," saith he, "hath God after so many ages now at last and so late bethought himself?"[3] Eusebius also writeth that Christian religion from the beginning for very spite was called νέα καὶ ξένη, that is to say, "new and strange."[4] After like sort these men condemn all our matters as strange and new; but they will have their own, whatsoever they are, to be praised as things of long continuance:[5] doing much like to the conjurers and sorcerers nowadays, which, working with devils, use to say they have their holy and hid mysteries from Athanasius, Cyprian, Moses, Abel, Adam, and from the Archangel Raphael, because that their cunning, being thought to come from such patrons and founders, might be judged the more high and holy. After the same fashion these men, because they would have their own religion, which they themselves, and that not long since, have brought forth into the world, to be the easilier and rather accepted of foolish persons, or of such as cast little whereabouts they or other do go, they are wont to say they had it from Augustine, Jerome, Chrysostom, from the apostles, and from Christ himself. Full well know they that nothing is more in the people's favor or better liketh the common sort than these names.

But how if the things which these men are so desirous to have seem new be found of greatest antiquity? Contrariwise, how

[2] [Acts 17:18–19.] [3] [Origen, *Contra Celsum,* bk. IV, ch. viii.]

[4] [Eusebius, *Church History,* bk. I, ch. iv.]

[5] [See "The Abstract of Chronicles Written" added to the *Defence* (1567) and later elaborated in the 1570 edition of the *Defence* in evidence of the antiquity of the English church and its customs (Jewel, *Works,* IV, 780–782).]

if all the things well nigh which they so greatly set out with the name of antiquity, having been well and thoroughly examined, be at length found to be but new and devised of very late? Soothly to say, no man that had a true and right consideration would think the Jews' laws and ceremonies to be new, for all Haman's accusation; for they were graven in very ancient tables of most antiquity. And although many did take Christ to have swerved from Abraham and the old fathers, and to have brought in a certain new religion in his own name, yet answered he them directly: "If ye believed Moses, ye would believe me also," for my doctrine is not so new as you make it; for Moses, an author of greatest antiquity, and one to whom ye give all honor, "hath spoken of me." [6] Paul likewise, though the Gospel of Jesus Christ be of many counted to be but new, yet hath it (saith he) the testimony most old both of the Law and prophets. As for our doctrine, which we may rightlier call Christ's catholic doctrine, it is so far off from new that God, who is above all most ancient and the Father of our Lord Jesus Christ, hath left the same unto us in the Gospel, in the prophets' and apostles' works, being monuments of greatest age. So that no man can now think our doctrine to be new unless the same think either the prophets' faith, or the Gospel, or else Christ himself to be new.

And as for their religion, if it be of so long continuance as they would have men ween it is, why do they not prove it so by the examples of the primitive church and by the fathers and councils of old times? Why lieth so ancient a cause thus long in the dust destitute of an advocate? Fire and sword they have had always ready at hand; but as for the old councils and the fathers, all mum, not a word. They did surely against all reason to begin first with these so bloody and extreme means if they could have found other more easy and gentle ways. And if they trust so fully to antiquity and use no dissimulation, why

[6] [John 5:46.]

did John Clement,[7] a countryman of ours, but few years past, in the presence of certain honest men and of good credit, tear and cast into the fire certain leaves of Theodoret the most ancient father and a Greek bishop, wherein he plainly and evidently taught that the nature of bread in the Communion was not changed, abolished, or brought to nothing? And this did he of purpose, because he thought there was no other copy thereof to be found. Why saith Albert Pighi that the ancient father Augustine had a wrong opinion of original sin; and that he erred and lied and used false logic as touching the case of matrimony concluded after a vow made, which Augustine affirmeth to be perfect matrimony indeed [8] and cannot be undone again? [9] Also, when they did of late put in print the ancient father Origen's work upon the Gospel of John, why left they quite out the whole sixth chapter, wherein it is likely, yea, rather of very surety, that the said Origen had written many things concerning the sacrament of the Holy Communion contrary to these men's minds, and would put forth that book mangled rather than full and perfect, for fear it should reprove them and their partners of their error? [10] Call ye this trusting to antiquity, when ye rent in pieces, keep back, maim, and burn the ancient fathers' works?

It is a world to see how well-favoredly and how towardly touching religion these men agree with the fathers, of whom they use to vaunt that they be their own good. The old council

[7] [John Clement (d. 1572), president of the College of Physicians and one of Wolsey's lecturers at Oxford. He was a recusant residing abroad during the reigns of Edward VI and Elizabeth I. Cf. *DNB,* under Clement, John.]

[8] Distinct. 27. Quidam. August. de bono vidu. cap. 10, 27, 41. Nuptiarum bonum. [Augustine, *De bono viduitatis,* ch. x. Cf. Jewel, *Works,* IV, 786, n. 14.]

[9] [Albertus Pighius, *Explic. Cathol. controv.,* Controv. I, f. 3.]

[10] Liber hodie extat et circumfertur mutilus. [For the interesting discussion of this, cf. Jewel, *Works,* IV, 789–790.]

Eliberine made a decree that nothing that is honored of the people should be painted in the churches.[11] The old father Epiphanius saith: "It is an horrible wickedness, and a sin not to be suffered, for any man to set up any pictures in the churches of the Christians, yea, though it were the picture of Christ himself."[12] Yet these men store all their temples and each corner of them with painted and carved images, as though without them religion were nothing worth.

The old fathers Origen[13] and Chrysostom[14] exhort the people to read the Scriptures, to buy them books, to reason at home among themselves of divine matters—wives with their husbands and parents with their children. These men condemn the Scriptures as dead elements and, as much as ever they may, bar the people from them. The ancient fathers Cyprian,[15] Epiphanius,[16] and Jerome say, "It is better for one who perchance has made a vow to lead a sole life, and afterward liveth unchastely, and cannot quench the flames of lust, to marry a wife and to live honestly in wedlock."[17] And the old father Augustine judgeth the selfsame marriage to be good and perfect and ought not to be broken again.[18] These men, if a man have once bound himself by a vow, though afterward he burn, keep queans, and defile himself with never so sinful and desperate a life, yet they suffer not that person to marry a wife; or, if he

[11] [*Concilia sacrosancta*, ed. Philip Labbei and Gabriel Cossartii (16 vols. in 17; Paris, 1671–1672), tom. I, col. 974, Concil. Elib., canon 36.]

[12] [Epiphanius, *Epist. ad Joannis episcopum Hierosolymitanum*, in Erasmus, *Hieronymi operum*, II, 156–157.]

[13] Orig. in Levit. ca. 16. [Origen, *In Leviticum*, hom. ix, ch. v.]

[14] [Chrysostom, *In Matthaeum*, hom. II, 29, 30, 31.] Idem in Johan. 31. [*In Johannem*, hom. xxxii.]

[15] Cypri. epist. II. Lib. i. [Cf. Cyprian, *Epist. IV, ad Pomponio fratri.*]

[16] [Epiphanius, *Adversus haereses*, bk. II, tom. I, haeresis lxi, *Adversus Apostolicos*, ch. vii.]

[17] [Jerome, *De servanda virginitate ad Demetriadem*, epist. CXXX.]

[18] [See p. 86 and note 8, above.]

chance to marry, they allow it not for marriage. And they commonly teach it is much better and more godly to keep a concubine and harlot than to live in that kind of marriage.

The old father Augustine complained of the multitude of vain ceremonies wherewith he even then saw men's minds and consciences overcharged.[19] These men, as though God regarded nothing else but their ceremonies, have so out of measure increased them that there is now almost none other thing left in their churches and places of prayer.

Again, that old father Augustine denieth it to be lawful for a monk to spend his time slothfully and idly and under a pretensed and counterfeit holiness to live all upon others.[20] And whoso thus liveth, an old father Apollonius likeneth him to a thief.[21] These men have, I wot not whether to name them droves or herds of monks, who for all they do nothing, nor yet once intend to bear any show of holiness, yet live they not only upon others, but also riot lavishly of other folks' labors.

The old council at Rome decreed that no man should come to the service said by a priest well known to keep a concubine.[22] These men let to farm concubines to their priests and yet constrain men by force against their will to hear their cursed paltry service.

The old canons of the apostles command that bishop to be removed from his office which will both supply the place of a civil magistrate and also of an ecclesiastical person.[23] These men, for all that, both do and will needs serve both places. Nay, rather, the one office which they ought chiefly to execute they

[19] [Augustine, *Ad inquisitiones Januarii,* liber secundus, epistola LV (alias 119), sec. 35.]

[20] [Augustine, *De opere monachorum,* chs. xii–xiii, xxii–xxv, etc. Cf. discussion of this citation in Jewel, *Works,* IV, 798–799 and notes.]

[21] [Socrates, *Church History,* bk. IV, ch. xxiii.]

[22] Concil. Rom. cap. 3. [Cf. Crabbe, *Concilia,* II, 765, Synod. Rom. under Nichol. I.]

[23] Canon 8. [Cf. *Concilia sacrosancta,* tom. I, col. 44, Canon. Apost. 82.]

once touch not, and yet nobody commandeth them to be displaced.

The old council Gangrense commandeth that none should make such difference between an unmarried priest and a married priest as he ought to think the one more holy than the other for single life sake.[24] These men put such a difference between them that they straightway think all their holy service to be defiled if it be done by a good and honest man that hath a wife.

The ancient Emperor Justinian commanded that in the holy administration all things should be pronounced with a clear, loud, and treatable voice, that the people might receive some fruit thereby.[25] These men, lest the people should understand them, mumble up all their service, not only with a drowned and hollow voice, but also in a strange and barbarous tongue.

The old council at Carthage commanded nothing to be read in Christ's congregation but the canonical Scriptures: [26] these men read such things in their churches as themselves know for a truth to be stark lies and fond fables.

But, if there be any that think that these above-rehearsed authorities be but weak and slender, because they were decreed by emperors and certain petty bishops, and not by so full and perfect councils, taking pleasure rather in the authority and name of the Pope; let such a one know that Pope Julius doth evidently forbid that a priest ministering the Communion should dip the bread in the cup.[27] These men, contrary to Pope Julius' decree, divide the bread and dip it in the wine.

Pope Clement saith it is not lawful for a bishop to deal with both swords; "For if thou wilt have both," saith he, "thou shalt

[24] [Cf. *Concilia sacrosancta,* tom. II, col. 419, Concil. Gangr., canon 4.]

[25] In Novel. Constitu. 123 & 146. [*Corpus juris civilis* (2 vols.; Amsterdam, 1663), II, 196–197, auth. coll. IX, tit. XX, novell. 137:6.]

[26] [Cf. Crabbe, *Concilia,* I, 431, Concil. Carthag. III, ch. xlvii.]

[27] [Cf. *Corpus juris canonici,* Decret. Gratian., Decr. Tert. Pars, De Consecr., Dist. ii, canon 7, col. 1914. Julius I was Pope from 337 to 352.]

deceive both thyself and those that obey thee."[28] Nowadays the Pope challengeth to himself both swords and useth both. Wherefore it ought to seem less marvel if that have followed which Clement saith, that is, "that he hath deceived both his own self and those which have given ear unto him."

Pope Leo saith upon one day it is lawful to say but one Mass in one church.[29] These men say daily in one church commonly ten Masses, twenty, thirty, yea, oftentimes more: so that the poor gazer-on can scant tell which way he was best to turn him.

Pope Gelasius saith it is a wicked deed and subject to sacrilege in any man to divide the Communion, and when he received one kind to abstain from the other.[30] These men, contrary to God's word and contrary to Pope Gelasius, command that one kind only of the Holy Communion be given to the people, and by so doing they make their priests guilty of sacrilege.

But if they will say that all these things are worn now out of ure and nigh dead, and pertain nothing to these present times; yet, to the end all folk may understand what faith is to be given to these men, and upon what hope they call together their said councils, let us see in few words what good heed they take to the selfsame things which they themselves these very last years (and the remembrance thereof is yet new and fresh) in their own general council that they had by order called, decreed and commanded to be devoutly kept. In the last council at Trent, scant fourteen years past, it was ordained by the com-

[28] [Cf. Crabbe, *Concilia,* I, 32, Clement ad Jacob, Epist. 1. This does not support Jewel, who admitted his error. Cf. Jewel, *Works,* IV, 819.]

[29] [Cf. Pope Leo I, *Epistola IX, ad Dioscorum Alexandrinum episcopum.* Jewel relies on the implications in this passage and not upon Leo's exact words.]

[30] [Cf. *Corpus juris canonici,* Decret. Gratian., Decr. Tert. Pars, De Consecr., Dist. ii, canon 12, col. 1918.]

mon consent of all degree that one man should not have two benefices at one time.[31] What is become now of that ordinance? Is the same too so soon worn out of mind and clean consumed? For these men, ye see, give to one man not two benefices only, but sundry abbeys many times, sometime also two bishoprics, sometime three, sometime four, and that not only to an unlearned man, but oftentimes even to a man of war.

In the said council a decree was made that all bishops should preach the Gospel.[32] These men neither preach nor once go up into the pulpit, neither think they it any part of their office. What great pomp and crack then is this they make of antiquity? Why brag they so of the names of the ancient fathers and of the new and old councils? Why will they seem to trust to their authority whom when they list they despise at their own pleasure?

But I have a special fancy to common a word or two rather with the Pope's good holiness and to say things to his own face. Tell us, I pray you, good Holy Father, seeing ye do crack so much of all antiquity and boast yourself that all men are bound to you alone, which of all the fathers have at any time called you by the name of the highest prelate, the universal bishop or head of the church? Which of them ever said that both the swords were committed to you? [33] Which of them ever said that you have authority and right to call councils? Which of them ever said that the whole world is your diocese? Which of them, that all bishops have received of your fullness? [34] Which of them, that all power is given to you as well in heaven as in earth? Which of them, that neither kings, nor the whole clergy, nor yet all people together, are able to be

[31] [Cf. *Concilia sacrosancta,* Decret. de Reform., ch. xvii, tom. XIV, col. 890, Concil. Trident, sess. xxiv.]

[32] [*Ibid.,* ch. iv, col. 883.]

[33] De Major. et obedientia. Unam Sanctam.

[34] [Cf. William Durandus (thirteenth-century papal official), *Rationale divinorum officiorum,* bk. II, ch. i., sec. 17.]

judges over you?[35] Which of them, that kings and emperors by Christ's commandment and will do receive authority at your hand? Which of them with so precise and mathematical limitation hath surveyed and determined you to be seventy and seven times greater than the mightiest kings?[36] Which of them, that more ample authority is given to you than to the residue of the patriarchs? Which of them, that you are the Lord God?[37] Or that you are not a mere natural man but a certain substance made and grown together of God and man?[38] Which of them, that you are the only headspring of all law? Which of them, that you have power over purgatories? Which of them, that you are able to command the angels of God as you list yourself? Which of them that ever said that you are Lord of lords and the King of kings?[39] We can also go further with you in like sort. What one amongst the whole number of the old bishops and fathers ever taught you either to say private Mass while the people stared on or to lift up the sacrament over your head (in which point consisteth now all your religion); or else to mangle Christ's sacraments and to bereave the people of the one part, contrary to Christ's institution and plain expressed words? But, that we may once come to an end, what one is there of all the fathers which hath taught you to distribute Christ's blood and the holy martyr's merits, and to sell openly as merchandises your pardons and all the rooms and lodgings of purgatory? These men are wont to speak much of a certain

[35] Concilium Lateranense. sub Jul. 2, Distinct. 9, Innocentij. [Cf. *Concilia sacrosancta,* tom. XIV, 5th Lateran Council. But see Jewel, *Works,* IV, 833.]

[36] De Major et obedien. Solitae. [Cf. Jewel, *Works,* IV, 837.]

[37] Extrv. Ioan 22. Cum inter. In Glosa in editione impressa parisiis, et Lugdum. [Cf. *Concilia sacrosancta,* tom. I, col. 268, and Jewel, *Works,* IV, 842.]

[38] Tit. vi. Gloss. in cap. 17, col. 132; Ibid. Clement. Lib. I, Gloss. in Proem. col. 4. [Cf. *Corpus juris canonici,* Sext. Decretal, bk. I.]

[39] Antonius de Rosellis.

secret doctrine of theirs and manifold and sundry readings. Then let them bring forth somewhat now, if they can, that it may appear they have at least read or do know somewhat. They have often stoutly noised in all corners where they went how all the parts of their religion be very old and have been approved not only by the multitude but also by the consent and continual observation of all nations and times. Let them therefore once in their life show this their antiquity. Let them make appear at eye that the things whereof they make such ado have taken so long and large increase. Let them declare that all Christian nations have agreed by consent to this their religion.

Nay, nay, they turn their backs, as we have said already, and flee from their own decrees, and have cut off and abolished again within a short space the same things which but a few years before themselves had established forevermore, forsooth, to continue. How should one then trust them in the fathers, in the old councils, and in the words spoken by God? They have not, good Lord, they have not (I say) those things which they boast they have: they have not that antiquity, they have not that universality, they have not that consent of all places nor of all times. And though they have a desire rather to dissemble, yet they themselves are not ignorant hereof: yea, and sometime also they let not to confess it openly. And for this cause they say that the ordinances of the old councils and fathers be such as may now and then be altered, and that sundry and divers decrees serve for sundry and divers times of the church. Thus lurk they under the name of the church and beguile silly creatures with their vain glozing. It is to be marveled that either men be so blind as they cannot see this, or, if they see it, to be so patient as they can so lightly and quietly bear it.

But, whereas they have commanded that those decrees should be void, as things now waxen too old and that have lost their grace, perhaps they have provided in their stead certain other better things and more profitable for the people. For it is a common saying with them that "if Christ himself or the apostles were alive again, they could not better nor godlier govern God's church than it is at this present governed by them." They have put somewhat in their stead indeed; but it is "chaff instead of wheat," as Jeremiah saith,[40] and such things as, according to Isaiah's words, "God never required at their hands." "They have stopped up," saith he, "all the veins of clear springing water, and have digged up for the people deceivable and puddle-like pits, full of mire and filth, which neither have nor are able to hold pure water."[41] They have plucked away from the people the Holy Communion, the word of God, from whence all comfort should be taken, the true worshiping of God also, and the right use of sacraments and prayer; and have given us of their own to play withal in the meanwhile salt, water, oil boxes, spittle, palms, bulls, jubilees, pardons, crosses, censings, and an endless rabble of ceremonies, and (as a man might term them with Plautus) pretty games to make sport withal. In these things have they set all their religion, teaching the people that by these God may be duly pacified, spirits be driven away, and men's consciences well quieted. For these, lo, be the orient colors and precious savors of Christian religion; these things doth God look upon and accepteth them thankfully; these must come in place to be honored and put quite away the institutions of Christ and his apostles. And like as in times past when wicked King Jeroboam had taken from the people the right serving of God and brought them to worship golden calves, lest perchance they might afterward change their mind and slip away, getting them again to Jerusalem to the temple of God there, he exhorted them with a long tale to be steadfast, saying thus unto them, "O Israel, these calves be thy gods";[42] in this sort commanded your God you should worship him; for it should be wearisome and troublous for you to take upon you

[40] [Jer. 23:28.] [41] [Isa. 1:12.] [42] [I Kings 12:28.]

a journey so far off and yearly to go up to Jerusalem there to serve and honor your God. Even after the same sort every whit, when these men had once made the law of God of none effect through their own traditions, fearing that the people should afterward open their eyes and fall another way, and should somewhence else seek a surer means of their salvation; Jesus, how often have they cried out, "This is the same worshiping that pleaseth God, and which he straitly requireth of us, and wherewith he will be turned from his wrath"; that by these things is conserved the unity of the church; by these all sins cleansed and consciences quieted; and whoso departeth from these hath left unto himself no hope of everlasting salvation? For it were wearisome and troublous (say they) for the people to resort to Christ, to the apostles, and to the ancient fathers, and to observe continually what their will and commandment should be. This, ye may see, is to withdraw the people of God from the weak elements of the world, from the leaven of the scribes and Pharisees, and from the traditions of men. It were reason, no doubt, that Christ's commandments and the apostles' were removed, that these their devices might come in place. O just cause, I promise you, why that ancient and so-long-allowed doctrine should be now abolished, and a new form of religion be brought into the church of God!

And yet, whatsoever it be, these men cry still that nothing ought to be changed; that men's minds are well satisfied herewithal; that the church of Rome, the church which cannot err, hath decreed these things. For Sylvester Prierias saith [43] that the Romish church is the squire and rule of truth, and that the Holy Scripture hath received from thence both authority and credit. "The doctrine," saith he, "of the Romish church is the rule of most infallible faith, from the which the Holy Scripture taketh his force." And "indulgences and pardons (saith he)

[43] [Sylvester Prierias, *Contra Luther. dialogus* ([n.p.], 1518), fund. 3. Prierias (1456–1523) was a Dominican and an opponent of Martin Luther.]

are not made known to us by the authority of the Scriptures, but they are known to us by the authority of the Romish church and of the bishops of Rome, which is greater than the Scriptures." Pighi also letteth not to say that without the license of the Romish church we ought not to believe the very plain Scriptures.[44] Much like as if any of those that cannot speak pure and clean Latin, and yet can babble out quickly and readily a little some such law Latin as serveth the court, would needs hold that all others ought also to speak after the same way which Mammotrectus and Catholicon [45] spake many years ago, and which themselves do yet use in pleading in court (for so may it be understood sufficiently what is said and men's desires be satisfied), and that it is a fondness now in the later end to trouble the world with a new kind of speaking and to call again the old fineness and eloquence that Cicero and Caesar used in their days in the Latin tongue. So much are these men beholden to the folly and darkness of the former times. "Many things," as one writeth, "are had in estimation oftentimes because they have been once dedicate to the temples of the heathen gods." Even so see we at this day many things allowed and highly set by of these men, not because they judge them so much worth, but only because they have been received into a custom and after a sort dedicate to the temple of God.

"Our church," say they, "cannot err." They speak that (I think) as the Lacedaemonians long since used to say that it was not possible to find any adulterer in all their commonwealth; whereas indeed they were rather all adulterers, and had no certainty in their marriages but had their wives common among them all. Or, as the canonists at this day, for their bellies' sake,

[44] [Pighius, *Hierarchiae ecclesiasticae assertio,* bk. I, ch. ii.]

[45] [Mammotrectus and Catholicon were aids for the students of Latin, both printed in the last half of the fifteenth century.]

use to say of the Pope,[46] that, forsomuch as he is lord of all benefices, though he sell for money bishoprics, monasteries, priesthood, spiritual promotions, and parts with nothing freely, yet because he counteth all his own, he cannot commit simony though he were never so fain. But how strongly and agreeably to reason these things be spoken we are not as yet able to perceive, except perchance these men have plucked off their wings from the truth, as the Romans in old time did proine and pinion their goddess Victory,[47] after they had once gotten her home, to the end that with the same wings she should never more be able to flee away from them again. But what if Jeremiah tell them, as is afore rehearsed, that these be lies? What if the same prophet say in another place that the selfsame men who ought to be keepers of the vineyard have brought to nought and destroyed the Lord's vineyard? How if Christ say that the same persons who chiefly ought to have a care over the temple have made of the Lord's temple a den of thieves? If it be so that the Church of Rome cannot err, it must needs follow that the good luck thereof is far greater than all these men's policy: for such is their life, their doctrine, and their diligence that for all them the church may not only err but also utterly be spoiled and perish. No doubt if that church may err which hath departed from God's word, from Christ's commandments, from the apostles' ordinances, from the primitive church's examples, from the old fathers' and councils' orders, and from their own

[46] Summa Angelica dictione Papa. [Cf. Angelus Carletus de Clavasio (fl. 1480), *Summa angelica de casibus conscientiae* (Strasbourg, 1513), in dict. Simonia, no. 6, fol. 271–272.] Theodoricus de Schismate. [Cf. Theodoricus de Niem (Dietrich von Nieheim) (fl. 1408), *De Schism. inter Urban VI, et Clement* (Basle, 1566), bk. II, ch. xxxii, p. 89.]

[47] Plutarchus. [This description has to do with the Athenians, not the Romans. See Pausanias (second-century Greek historian), *Accurata Graeciae descriptio* (Leipzig, 1696), bk. III, 245. "Proine and pinion" in this place means to prune and clip the wings of the goddess.]

decrees, and which will be bound within the compass of none, neither old nor new, nor their own, nor other folks', nor man's law, nor God's law; then it is out of all question that the Romish church hath not only had power to err but that it hath shamefully and most wickedly erred in very deed.

But, say they, ye have been once of our fellowship, but now ye are become forsakers of your profession and have departed from us. It is true we have departed from them, and for so doing we both give thanks to Almighty God and greatly rejoice on our own behalf. But yet for all this, from the primitive church, from the apostles, and from Christ, we have not departed. True it is, we were brought up with these men in darkness and in the lack of knowledge of God, as Moses was taught up in the learning and the bosom of the Egyptians. "We have been of your company," saith Tertullian, "I confess it, and no marvel at all; for," saith he, "men be made and not born Christians."[48] But wherefore, I pray you, have they themself, the citizens and dwellers of Rome, removed and come down from those seven hills whereupon Rome sometime stood to dwell rather in the plain called Mars his field? They will say, peradventure, because the conducts of water, wherewithout men cannot commodiously live, have now failed and are dried up in those hills. Well then, let them give us like leave in seeking the water of eternal life that they give themselves in seeking the water of the well. For the water verily failed amongst them. "The elders of the Jews," saith Jeremiah, "sent their little ones to the waterings; and they, finding no water, being in a miserable case and utterly marred for thirst, brought home again their vessels empty."[49] "The needy and poor folk," saith Isaiah, "sought about for water, but nowhere found they any; their tongue was even withered for thirst."[50] Even so these men have broken in pieces all the pipes and conduits: they have stopped up all the

[48] [Tertullian, *Apology,* ch. xviii.]
[49] [Jer. 14:3.]
[50] [Isa. 41:17.]

springs and choked up the fountain of living water with dirt and mire. And as Caligula many years past locked fast up all the storehouses of corn in Rome and thereby brought a general dearth and famine amongst the people; even so these men, by damming up all the fountains of God's word, have brought the people into a pitiful thirst. They have brought into the world, as saith the prophet Amos, "a hunger and a thirst; not the hunger of bread, nor the thirst of water, but of hearing the word of God." [51] With great distress went they scattering about, seeking some spark of heavenly light to refresh their consciences withal; but that light was already thoroughly quenched out, so that they could find none. This was a rueful state: this was a lamentable form of God's church. It was a misery to live therein, without the Gospel, without light, and without all comfort.

Wherefore, though our departing were a trouble to them, yet ought they to consider withal how just cause we had of our departure. For if they will say it is in no wise lawful for one to leave the fellowship wherein he has been brought up, they may as well in our names, and upon our heads, condemn both the prophets, the apostles, and Christ himself. For why complain they not also of this, that Lot went quite his way out of Sodom, Abraham out of Chaldee, the Israelites out of Egypt, Christ from the Jews, and Paul from the Pharisees? For, except it be possible there may be a lawful cause of departing, we see no reason why Lot, Abraham, the Israelites, Christ, and Paul may not be accused of sects and sedition as well as others.

And if these men will needs condemn us for heretics because we do not all things at their commandment, whom (in God's name) or what kind of men ought they themselves to be taken for which despise the commandment of Christ and of the apostles? If we be schismatics because we have left them, by what name shall they call themselves which have forsaken the Greeks, from whom they first received their faith, forsaken the primi-

[51] [Amos 8:11.]

tive church, forsaken Christ himself and the apostles, even as children should forsake their parents? For though those Greeks who at this day profess religion and Christ's name have many things corrupt amongst them, yet hold they still a great number of those things which they received from the apostles. They have neither private Masses, nor mangled sacraments, nor purgatories, nor pardons. And as for the titles of high bishops and those glorious names, they esteem them so as, whosoever he were that would take upon him the same and would be called either universal bishop or the head of the universal church, they make no doubt to call such a one both a passing proud man, a man that works despite against all the other bishops his brethren, and a plain heretic.

Now then, since it is manifest and out of all peradventure that these men are fallen from the Greeks, of whom they received the Gospel, of whom they received the faith, the true religion, and the church; what is the matter why they will not now be called home again to the same men, as it were to their originals and first founders? And why be they afraid to take a pattern of the apostles' and old fathers' times, as though they all had been void of understanding? Do these men, ween ye, see more, or set more by the church of God than they did who first delivered us these things?

We truly have renounced that church wherein we could neither have the word of God sincerely taught, nor the sacraments rightly administered, nor the name of God duly called upon; which church also themselves confess to be faulty in many points; and wherein was nothing able to stay any wise man or one that has consideration of his own safety. To conclude, we have forsaken the church as it is now, not as it was in old time, and have so gone from it as Daniel went out of the lions' den and the three children out of the furnace; and, to say truth, we have been cast out by these men (being cursed of them, as they use to say, with book, bell, and candle) rather than have gone away from them of ourselves.

And we are come to that church wherein they themselves cannot deny (if they will say truly and as they think in their own conscience) but all things be governed purely and reverently and, as much as we possibly could, very near to the order used in the old time.

Let them compare our churches and theirs together and they shall see that themselves have most shamefully gone from the apostles and we most justly have gone from them. For we, following the example of Christ, of the apostles and the holy fathers, give the people the Holy Communion whole and perfect; but these men, contrary to all the fathers, to all the apostles, and contrary to Christ himself, do sever the sacraments and pluck away the one part from the people, and that with most notorious sacrilege, as Gelasius termeth it.[52]

We have brought again the Lord's Supper unto Christ's institution, and will have it to be a communion in very deed, common and indifferent to a great number, according to the name. But these men have changed all things, contrary to Christ's institution, and have made a private Mass of the Holy Communion. And so it cometh to pass that we give the Lord's Supper unto the people and they give them a vain pageant to gaze upon.

We affirm, together with the ancient fathers, that the body of Christ is not eaten but of the good and faithful and of those that are endued with the Spirit of Christ. Their doctrine is that Christ's very body effectually and, as they speak, really and substantially may not only be eaten of the wicked and unfaithful men but also (which is monstrous to be spoken) of mice and dogs.

[52] [*Corpus juris canonici,* Decret. Gratian., Decr. Tert. Pars, De Consecr, Dist. ii, canon 12, col. 1918.]

We use to pray in church after that fashion as, according to Paul's lesson,[53] the people may know what we pray, and may answer Amen with a general consent. These men, like sounding metal, yell out in the churches unknown and strange words without understanding, without knowledge, and without devotion; yea, and do it of purpose because the people should understand nothing at all.

But, not to tarry about rehearsing all points wherein we and they differ (for they have well nigh no end), we turn the Scriptures into all tongues; they scant suffer them to be had abroad in any tongue. We allure the people to read and to hear God's word; they drive the people from it. We desire to have our cause known to all the world; they flee to come to any trial. We lean unto knowledge; they unto ignorance. We trust unto light; they unto darkness. We reverence, as it becometh us, the writings of the apostles and prophets; and they burn them. Finally, we in God's cause desire to stand to God's only judgment; they will stand only to their own. Wherefore, if they will weigh all these things with a quiet mind and fully bent to hear and to learn, they will not only allow this determination of ours, who have forsaken errors and followed Christ and his apostles, but themselves also will forsake their own selves and join of their own accord to our side.

[53] I Cor. 14 [:16].

# Part VI

BUT peradventure they will say it was treason to attempt these matters without a sacred general council; for in that consists the whole force of the church: there Christ hath promised he will ever be a present assistant. Yet they themselves, without tarrying for any general council, have broken the commandments of God and the decrees of the apostles; and, as we said a little above, they have spoiled and disannulled almost all, not only ordinances, but even the doctrine of the primitive church. And where they say it is not lawful to make a change without a council, what was he that gave us these laws, or from whence had they this injunction?

King Agesilaus truly did but fondly, who, when he had a determinate answer made him of the opinion and will of mighty Jupiter, would afterward bring the whole matter before Apollo, to know whether he allowed thereof as his father Jupiter did or no.[1] But yet should we do much more fondly, when we may hear God himself plainly speak to us in the most Holy Scriptures, and may understand by them his will and meaning, if we would afterward (as though this were of none effect) bring our whole cause to be tried by a council; which were nothing else but to ask whether men would allow as God did, and

[1] Plutarchus.

whether men would confirm God's commandment by their authority. Why, I beseech you, except a council will and command, shall not truth be truth or God be God? If Christ had meant to do so from the beginning, as that he would preach or teach nothing without the bishops' consent but refer all his doctrine over to Annas and Caiaphas, where should now have been the Christian faith, or who at any time should have heard the Gospel taught? Peter, verily, whom the Pope hath oftener in his mouth and more reverently useth to speak of than he doth of Jesus Christ, did boldly stand against the holy council, saying, "It is better to obey God than men." [2] And after Paul had once entirely embraced the Gospel, and had received it, "not from men, nor by man, but by the only will of God," he did not take advice therein of flesh and blood, nor brought the case before his kinsmen and brethren but went forthwith into Arabia, to preach God's divine mysteries by God's only authority.[3]

Yet truly we do not despise councils, assemblies, and conferences of bishops and learned men; neither have we done that we have done altogether without bishops or without a council. The matter hath been treated in open parliament, with long consultation and before a notable synod and convocation.[4]

But touching this council which is now summoned by the Pope Pius, wherein men so lightly are condemned which have been neither called, heard, nor seen, it is easy to guess what we may look for or hope of it. In times past, when Nazianzene saw in his days how men in such assemblies were so blind and willful that they were carried with affections and labored more to get the victory than the truth, he pronounced openly that he never had seen a good end of any council.[5] What would he say

[2] [Acts 4:19.] [3] [Gal. 1:12.]

[4] [Reference to the first Elizabethan parliament and convocation (1559).]

[5] [Cf. Gregory of Nazianzus, *Epistola CXXX, ad Procopio.*]

now, if he were alive at this day and understood the heaving and shoving of these men? For at that time, though the matter were labored on all sides, yet the controversies were well heard and open errors were put clean away by the general voice of all parts. But these men will neither have the case to be freely disputed, nor yet, how many errors soever there be, suffer they any to be changed. For it is a common custom of theirs often and shamelessly to boast that their church cannot err, that in it there is no fault, and that they must give place to us in nothing. Or if there be any fault, yet must it be tried by their bishops and abbots only, because they be the directors and rulers of matters, and they be the church of God. Aristotle saith that a "city cannot consist of bastards"; but whether the church of God may consist of these men, let their own selves consider. For doubtless, neither be the abbots legitimate abbots, nor the bishops natural right bishops. But grant they be the church; let them be heard speak in councils; let them alone have authority to give consent; yet in old time, when the church of God (if ye will compare it with their church) was very well governed, both elders and deacons, as saith Cyprian,[6] and certain also of the common people, were called thereunto and made acquainted with ecclesiastical matters.

But I put case, these abbots and bishops have no knowledge: what if they understand nothing what religion is nor how we ought to think of God? I put case, the pronouncing and ministering of the law be decayed in priests, and good counsel fail in the elders, and, as the prophet Micah saith, "the night be unto them instead of a vision, and darkness instead of prophesying"; [7] or, as Isaiah saith, what if all "the watchmen of the city are become blind"? [8] What "if the salt have lost his proper strength

[6] [Cyprian, *Epistola XIV, Presbyteris et Diaconis Fratribus,* final paragraph.]

[7] [Mic. 3:6.] [8] [Isa. 56:10.]

and savoriness" and, as Christ saith, "be good for no use, scant worth the casting on the dunghill"? [9]

Well, yet then, they will bring all matters before the Pope, who cannot err. To this I say, first, it is a madness to think that the Holy Ghost taketh his flight from a general council to run to Rome, to the end, if he doubt or stick in any matter and cannot expound it of himself, he may take counsel of some other spirit, I wot not what, that is better learned than himself. For, if this be true, what needed so many bishops, with so great charges and so far journeys, have assembled their convocation at this present at Trent? It had been more wisdom and better, at least it had been a much nearer way and handsomer, to have brought all things rather before the Pope and to have come straight forth and have asked counsel at his divine breast. Secondly, it is also an unlawful dealing to toss our matter from so many bishops and abbots and to bring it at last to the trial of one only man, specially of him who himself is appeached by us of heinous and foul enormities and has not yet put in his answer; who had also aforehand condemned us without judgment by order pronounced and or ever we were called to be judged.

How say ye, do we devise these tales? Is not this the course of the councils in these days? Are not all things removed from the whole holy council and brought before the Pope alone; that, as though nothing had been done to purpose by the judgments and consents of such a number, he alone may add, alter, diminish, disannul, allow, remit, and qualify whatsoever he list? Whose words be these then? And why have the bishops and abbots, in the last Council at Trent, but of late concluded with saying thus in the end: "Saving always the authority of the see apostolic in all things"? Or why doth Pope Paschal write so proudly of himself? "As though," saith he, "there were any

[9] [Matt. 5:13; Luke 14:35.]

general council able to prescribe a law to the Church of Rome; whereas all councils both have been made and have received their force and strength by the Church of Rome's authority; and in ordinances made by councils is ever plainly excepted the authority of the Bishop of Rome."[10] If they will have these things allowed for good, why be councils called? But if they command them to be void, why are they left in their books as things allowable?

But be it so. Let the Bishop of Rome alone be above all councils, that is to say, let some one part be greater than the whole, let him be of greater power, let him be of more wisdom than all his, and, in spite of Jerome's head, let the authority of one city be greater than the authority of the whole world.[11] How then, if the Pope have seen none of these things, and have never read either the Scriptures, or the old fathers, or yet his own councils? How if he favor the Arians, as once Pope Liberius did,[12] or have a wicked and a detestable opinion of the life to come and of the immortality of the soul, as Pope John had but few years since,[13] or, to increase now his own dignity, do corrupt other councils, as Pope Zosimus corrupted the council holden at Nicaea in times past,[14] and do say that these things were devised and appointed by the holy fathers, which never once came into their thought, and, to have the full sway of authority, do wrest the Scriptures, which thing as Camotensis

[10] De Electioni et Electi potestate ca. significasti. [Cf. *Corpus juris canonici,* Decret. Gregor. IX, bk. I, tit. vi., ch. iv, cols. 111–112. Paschal II was Pope from 1099 to 1118.]

[11] Hieron. ad Evagrium. [Jerome, *Epist. ad Euagrium,* in *Hieronymi operum,* II, 330.]

[12] [Cf. Sozomen, *Church History,* bk. IV, ch. xv.]

[13] [Jewel cites Jean Gerson, *Sermo in Fest. Pasch.,* in support here. Cf. Jewel, *Works,* IV, 930. It would seem that Jewel has reference to Basassare Cossa, John XXIII, antipope from 1410 to 1415.]

[14] [Cf. Jewel, *Works,* IV, 937 and notes.]

saith is an unusual custom with the popes? [15] How if he have renounced the faith in Christ and become an apostate, as Lyra saith many popes have been? [16] And yet, for all this, shall the Holy Ghost with turning of a hand knock at his breast, and even whether he will or no, yea, and wholly against his will, kindle him a light so as he may not err? Shall he straightway be the headspring of all right, and shall all treasure of wisdom and understanding be found in him, as it were laid up in store? Or, if these things be not in him, can he give a right and apt judgment of so weighty matters? Or, if he be not able to judge, would he have that all those matters should be brought before him alone?

What will ye say if the Pope's advocates, abbots and bishops, dissemble not the matter, but show themselves open enemies to the Gospel, and though they see, yet they will not see, but wry the Scriptures and wittingly and knowingly corrupt and counterfeit the word of God, and foully and wickedly apply to the Pope all the same things which evidently and properly be spoken of the person of Christ only nor by no means can be applied to any other? And what though they say "the Pope is all and above all"? Or that "he can do as much as Christ can" and that "one judgment place and one council house serve for the Pope and for Christ both together"? [17] Or "that the Pope is the same light which should come into the world," which words

[15] [Cf. Heinrich Cornelius Agrippa von Nettesheim, *De incertitudine et vanitate scientiarum et artium* (Cologne, 1584), ch. xcii, fol. Z.3.2. Concerning the identity of Camotensis, whom Jewel believed to be John of Salisbury, twelfth-century philosopher, see Jewel, *Works,* IV, 938 and n. 7.]

[16] [Nicholas Lyra (Franciscan scholar of the early fifteenth century), *Biblia cum. gloss. ord. et. expos.* (Basle, 1502), Matt. 16, pars V, fol. 52.]

[17] Host. Cap. Quarto. [Henricus de Segusio Hostiensis (cardinal who flourished about 1262), *Sup. decretal, comm.* (Paris, 1512), tit. vii, *De Transl. Episc.,* ch. iii, fol. 75]; Abb. Pan. de Elect. cap. Venerabilis. [Panormitanus (Benedictine abbot and canonist, d. 1445), *Sup. decretal* (Lyons, 1534), tit. vi, De Elect., ch. xxxiv, fol. 156.]

Christ spake of himself alone;[18] and that "whoso is an evil-doer hateth and flieth from that light"?[19] Or that "all the other bishops have received of the Pope's fullness"?[20] Shortly, what though they make decrees expressly against God's word, and that not in huckermucker or covertly but openly and in the face of the world, must it needs yet be gospel straight whatsoever these men say? Shall these be God's holy army, or will Christ be at hand among them there? Shall the Holy Ghost flow in their tongues, or can they with truth say, "We and the Holy Ghost have thought good so"? Indeed Peter Asotus[21] and his companion Hosius[22] stick not to affirm that the same council wherein our Saviour Jesus Christ was condemned to die had both the spirit of prophesying and the Holy Ghost and the spirit of truth in it; and that it was neither a false nor a trifling saying when those bishops said, "We have a law, and by our law he ought to die";[23] and that "they, so saying, did light upon the very truth of judgment"; for so be Hosius' words; and that the same plainly was a just decree whereby they pronounced that Christ was worthy to die. This, methinketh, is strange, that these men are not able to speak for themselves and defend their own cause, but they must also take part with Annas and Caiaphas. For, if they will call that a lawful and good council wherein the Son of God was most shamefully condemned to die, what council will they then allow for false and naught?

[18] [John 8:12.]

[19] Corn. Episc. in Conc. Trid. [Cornelius (sixteenth-century Bishop of Bitonto), *Oratio ad Concil. Trident.*, in *Concilia sacrosancta,* tom. XIV, col. 996.]

[20] Durandus. [Durandus, *Rationale divinorum officiorum,* bk. II, ch. i, sec. 17.]

[21] [Harding was offended that Lady Bacon translated the *Peter a Soto* of the Latin as "Peter Asotus," *asotus* meaning "a worthless and debauched character." Cf. Jewel, *Works,* IV, 941.]

[22] Hosius contr. Brentium. Lib. 2. [Cf. Hosius, *Contra Brentius* (Cologne, 1558), bk. II, and Jewel, *Works,* IV, 941–942.]

[23] [John 8:12.]

And yet (as all their councils, to say truth, commonly be) necessity compelled them to pronounce these things to the council holden by Annas and Caiaphas.

But will these men (I say) reform us the church, being themselves both the persons guilty and the judges too? Will they abate their own ambition and pride? Will they overthrow their own causes and give sentence against themselves that they must leave off to be unlearned bishops, slow bellies, heapers together of benefices, takers upon them as princes and men of war? Will the abbots, the Pope's dear darlings, judge that monk for a thief which laboreth not for his living? And that it is against all law to suffer such a one to live and to be found either in city or in country, or all of other men's charges? Or else, that a monk ought to lie on the ground, to live hardly with herbs and peason,[24] to study earnestly, to argue, to pray, to work with hand, and fully to bend himself to come to the ministry of the church? In faith, as soon will the Pharisees and scribes repair again the temple of God and restore it unto us a house of prayer instead of a thievish den.

There have been, I know, certain of their own companions which have found fault with many errors of the church, as Pope Hadrian, Aeneas Silvius, Cardinal Pole, Pighi, and others, as is aforesaid: they held afterward their council at Trent, in the selfsame place where it is now appointed. There assembled many bishops and abbots and others whom it behooved for that matter. They were alone by themselves; whatsoever they did nobody gainsaid it, for they had quite shut out and barred our side from all manner of assemblies; and there they sat six years feeding folks with a marvelous expectation of their doings. The first six months, as though it were greatly needful, they made many determinations of the Holy Trinity, of the Father, of the Son, and of the Holy Ghost, which were godly things indeed but not so necessary for that time. Let us see, in all

[24] [I.e., peas.]

that while, of so many, so manifest, so often confessed by them, and so evident errors, what one error have they amended? From what kind of idolatry have they reclaimed the people? What superstition have they taken away? What piece of their tyranny and pomp have they diminished? As though all the world may not now see that this is a conspiracy and not a council; and that these bishops, whom the Pope hath now called together, be wholly sworn and become bound to bear him their faithful allegiance and will do no manner of thing but that they perceive pleaseth him and helpeth to advance his power and as he will have it; or that they reckon not of the number of men's voices rather than of the weight and value of the same; or that might doth not oftentimes overcome the right.

And therefore we know that divers times many good men and catholic bishops did tarry at home and would not come when such councils were called, wherein men so apparently labored to serve factions and to take parts, because they knew they should but lose their travail and do no good, seeing whereunto their enemies' minds were so wholly bent. Athanasius denied to come when he was called by the Emperor to his council at Caesarea, perceiving plain he should but come among his enemies which deadly hated him.[25] The same Athanasius, when he came afterward to the council at Syrmium and foresaw what would be the end by reason of the outrage and malice of his enemies, he packed up his carriage and went away immediately. John Chrysostom, although the Emperor Constantius [26] commanded him by four sundry letters to come to the Arians' council, yet kept he himself at home still.[27] When Maximus, the Bishop of Jerusalem, sat in the council at Palestine, the old

[25] [Theodoret, *Historia ecclesiastica,* bk. I, ch. xxviii.]

[26] [The Emperor Arcadio is meant here, as the Latin correctly indicates.]

[27] Tripartita. Hist. lib. 10. cap. 13. [Cassiodorus, *Tripartita historia* (Paris, [n.d.]), bk. X, ch. xiii.]

father Paphnutius took him by the hand and led him out at the doors, saying, "It is not lawful for us to confer of these matters with wicked men."[28] The bishops of the East would not come to the Syrmian council after they knew Athanasius had gotten himself thence again. Cyril called men back by letters from the council of them which were named Patropassians. Paulinus, Bishop of Trier, and many others more refused to come to the council at Milan when they understood what a stir and rule Auxentius kept there;[29] for they saw it was in vain to go thither where not reason but faction should prevail, and where folk contended not for the truth and right judgment of the matter but for partiality and favor.

And yet, for all those fathers had such malicious and stiff-necked enemies, yet if they had come they should have had free speech at least in the councils. But now, sithence, none of us may be suffered so much as to sit, or once to be seen in these men's meetings, much less suffered to speak freely our mind; and seeing the Pope's legates, patriarchs, archbishops, bishops, and abbots, all being conspired together, all linked together in one kind of fault, and all bound by one oath, sit alone by themselves and have power alone to give their consent; and at last, when they have all done, as though they had done nothing, bring all their opinions to be judged at the will and pleasure of the Pope, being but one man, to the end he may pronounce his own sentence of himself who ought rather to have answered to his complaint; sithence also the same ancient and Christian liberty, which of all right should specially be in Christian councils, is now utterly taken away from the council—for these causes, I say, wise and good men ought not to marvel at this day though we do the like now that they see

[28] Euseb. lib. 1. cap. 17. [The *Defence* refers to Rufinus here as the source, which is correct. Cf. Rufinus, *Church History*, bk. X, ch. xvii.]

[29] Sozomenus lib. 5. cap. 1. [Cf. Socrates, *Church History*, bk. II, ch. xxxvi.]

was done in times past in like case of so many fathers and catholic bishops; which is as though we choose rather to sit at home and leave our whole cause to God than to journey thither; whereas we neither shall have place nor be able to do any good; whereas we can obtain no audience; whereas princes' ambassadors be but used as mockingstocks; and whereas also we be condemned already, before trial, as though the matter were aforehand dispatched and agreed upon.

Nevertheless, we can bear patiently and quietly our own private wrongs. But wherefore do they shut out Christian kings and good princes from their convocation? Why do they so uncourteously, or with such spite, leave them out, and, as though they were not either Christian men or else could not judge, will not have them made acquainted with the cause of Christian religion, nor understand the state of their own churches?

Or, if the said kings and princes happen to intermeddle in such matters and take upon them to do that they may do, that they be commanded to do, and ought of duty to do, and the same things that we know both David and Solomon and other good princes have done, that is, if they, whiles the Pope and his prelates slug and sleep or else mischievously withstand them, do bridle the priests' sensuality and drive them to do their duty and keep them still to it; if they do overthrow idols; if they take away superstition and set up again the true worshiping of God; why do they by and by make an outcry upon them that such princes trouble all and press by violence into another body's office, and do thereby wickedly and malapertly? What Scripture hath at any time forbidden a Christian prince to be made privy to such causes? Who but themselves alone made ever any such law?

They will say to this, I guess, civil princes have learned to govern a commonwealth and to order matters of war but they understand not the secret mysteries of religion. If that be so, what is the Pope, I pray you, at this day other than a monarch or a prince? Or what be the cardinals, who must be none other nowadays but princes' and kings' sons? What else be the patriarchs and, for the most part, the archbishops, the bishops, the abbots? What be they else at this present in the Pope's kingdom but worldly princes, but dukes and earls, gorgeously accompanied with bands of men whithersoever they go, oftentimes also gaily arrayed with chains and collars of gold? They have at times, too, certain ornaments by themselves, as crosses, pillars, hats, miters, and palls, which pomp the ancient bishops Chrysostom, Augustine, and Ambrose never had. Setting these things aside, what teach they? What say they? What do they? How live they, I say not, as may become a bishop, but as may become even a Christian man? Is it so great a matter to have a vain title and by changing a garment only to have the name of a bishop?

Surely to have the principal stay and effect of all matters committed wholly to these men's hands, who neither know nor will know these things, nor yet set a jot by any point of religion save that which concerns their belly and riot; and to have them alone sit as judges and to be set up as overseers in the watch-tower, being no better than blind spies; of the other side, to have a Christian prince of good understanding and of a right judgment to stand still like a block of a stake, not to be suffered neither to give his voice nor to show his judgment, but only to wait what these men shall will and command, as one which had neither ears, nor eyes, nor wit, nor heart; and, whatsoever they give in charge, to allow it without exception, blindly fulfilling their commandments be they never so blasphemous and wicked, yea, although they command him quite to destroy all religion and to crucify again Christ himself—this surely, besides that it is proud and spiteful, is also beyond all right and reason and not to be endured of Christian and wise princes. Why, I pray you, may Caiaphas and Annas understand these matters, and may not David and Hezekiah do the same? Is it lawful for a cardinal, being a man of war, and delightious in blood, to have a place in a council, and is it not lawful for a Christian emperor or a king? We truly grant no further liberty to our magistrates than that we know hath both been given them by the word of God and also confirmed by the examples of the very best governed commonwealths. For, besides that a Christian prince hath the charge of both tables committed to him by God, to the end he may understand that not temporal matters only but also religious and ecclesiastical causes pertain to his office; besides also that God by his prophets often and earnestly commandeth the king to cut down the groves, to break down the images and altars of idols, and to write out the book of the law for himself; and besides that the prophet Isaiah saith, "A king ought to be a patron and nurse of the church"; [30] I say, besides all these things, we see by histories and by examples of the best times that good princes ever took the administration of ecclesiastical matters to pertain to their duty.

Moses, a civil magistrate and chief guide of the people, both received from God and delivered to the people all the order for religion and sacrifices, and gave Aaron the bishop a vehement and sore rebuke for making the golden calf and for suffering the corruption of religion.[31] Joshua also, though he were none other than a civil magistrate, yet as soon as he was chosen by God and set as a ruler over the people, he received commandments specially touching religion and the service of God.[32] King David, when the whole religion was altogether brought out of frame by wicked King Saul, brought home again the ark of God, that is to say, he restored religion again, and was not only amongst them himself as a counselor and furtherer of the work, but he appointed also hymns and psalms, put in order the

[30] [Isa. 49:23.] [31] Exod. 32[:21]. [32] Joshua ca. 1.

companies, and was the only doer in setting forth that whole solemn triumph, and in effect ruled the priests.[33] King Solomon built unto the Lord the temple which his father David had but purposed in his mind to do; and, after the finishing thereof, he made a godly oration to the people concerning religion and the service of God: [34] he afterward displaced Abiathar the priest and set Sadok in his place.[35] After this, when the temple of God was in shameful wise polluted through the naughtiness and negligence of the priests, King Hezekiah commanded the same to be cleansed from the rubble and filth,[36] the priests to light up the candles, to burn incense, and to do their divine service according to the old allowed custom. The same king also commanded the brazen serpent, which then the people wickedly worshiped, to be taken down and beaten to powder.[37] King Jehoshaphat overthrew and utterly made away the hill altars and groves,[38] whereby he saw God's honor hindered and the people holden back with a private superstition from the ordinary temple which was at Jerusalem, whereto they should by order have resorted yearly from every part of the realm. King Josiah with great diligence put the priests and bishops in mind of their duty.[39] King Joash bridled the riot and arrogancy of the priests.[40] Jehu put to death the wicked prophets.[41]

And, to rehearse no more examples out of the old law, let us rather consider, since the birth of Christ, how the church hath been governed in the Gospel's time. The Christian emperors in old time appointed the councils of the bishops. Constantine called the Council of Nicaea. Theodosius the First called the council at Constantinople. Theodosius the Second, the council at Ephesus. Marcian, the council at Chalcedon.

[33] 1 Paral [I Chron.] 13.
[34] 2 Paral [II Chron.] 6.
[35] [I Kings 2:26, 27, 35.]
[36] 2 Paral 29 [II Chron. 29:5].
[37] 4 Regis 18 [II Kings 18:4].
[38] 2 Paral 17 [II Chron. 17:6].
[39] 4 Regum 23 [II Kings 23:20].
[40] 4 Regum 12 [II Kings 12:7].
[41] 4 Regum 10 [II Kings 10:25].

And, when Rufinus the heretic had alleged for authority a council, which, as he thought, should make for him, Jerome his adversary, to confute him, "Tell us," quod he, "what emperor commanded that council to be called?"[42] The same Jerome again, in his epitaph upon Paula, maketh mention of the Emperor's letters, which gave commandment to call the bishops of Italy and Greece to Rome to a council.[43] Continually, for the space of five hundred years, the Emperor alone appointed the ecclesiastical assemblies and called the councils of the bishops together.

We now therefore marvel the more at the unreasonable dealing of the Bishop of Rome, who, knowing what was the Emperor's right when the church was well ordered, knowing also that it is now a common right to all princes, forsomuch as kings are now fully possessed in the several parts of the whole empire, doth so without consideration assign that office alone to himself, and taketh it sufficient, in summoning a general council, to make a man that is prince of the whole world no otherwise partaker thereof than he would make his own servant.[44] And although the modesty and mildness of the Emperor Ferdinand be so great that he can bear this wrong, because peradventure he understandeth not well the Pope's packing, yet ought not the Pope of his holiness to offer him that wrong nor to claim as his own another man's right.

But hereto some will reply, "The Emperor indeed called councils at that time ye speak of, because the Bishop of Rome was not yet grown so great as he is now; but yet the Emperor did not then sit together with the bishops in council, or once bare any stroke with his authority in their consultation." I answer, Nay, that it is not so; for, as witnesses Theodoret, the

[42] [Jerome, *Apologia adversus libros Rufini,* bk. II.]

[43] [Jerome, *Epistola ad Eustochium, Epitaphium Paulae matris.*]

[44] Ita pius 4 in bulla sua ad Imperat. Ferdinandum. [Cf. Pius IV, Bull, 3 Kal., Dec., 1560.]

Emperor Constantine sat not only together with them in the council at Nicaea but gave also advice to the bishops how it was best to try out the matter by the apostles' and prophets' writings, as appeareth by these his own words: "In disputation," saith he, "of matters of divinity, we have set before us to follow the doctrine of the Holy Ghost. For the evangelists' and the apostles' works, and the prophets' sayings, show us sufficiently what opinion we ought to have of the will of God." [45] The Emperor Theodosius (as saith Socrates) did not only sit among the bishops but also ordered the whole arguing of the cause, and tare in pieces the heretics' books, and allowed for good the judgment of the catholics.[46] In the Council of Chalcedon a civil magistrate condemned for heretics, by the sentence of his own mouth, the bishops Dioscorus, Juvenal, and Thalasius, and gave judgment to put them down from their dignities in the church.[47] In the third council at Constantinople, Constantine, a civil magistrate, did not only sit amongst the bishops, but did also subscribe with them: for saith he, "We have both read and subscribed." [48] In the second council called Arausicanum the princes' ambassadors, being noblemen born, not only spake their mind touching religion but set to their hands also, as well as the bishops. For thus is it written in the later end of that council: "Petrus, Marcellinus, Felix, and Liberius, being most noble men and the famous lieutenants and captains of France, and also peers of the realm, have given their consent and set to their hands." Further: "Syagrius, Opilio, Pantagathus, Deodatus, Cariattho, and Marcellus, men of very great honor, have subscribed." [49] If it be so then that lieutenants, chief cap-

[45] Hist. Eccli. lib. 1, cap. 5. (Cf. Theodoret, *Hist. eccles.*, bk. I, ch. vii.]

[46] Socrat. lib. 1. cap. 5. [Socrates, *Church History*, bk. I, ch. v.]

[47] Socrat. lib. 5., cap. 10. [*Ibid.*, bk. V, ch. x.]

[48] Actions 2. [Cf. *Concilia sacrosancta*, tom. VI, col. 1098, Edict. Imp. Constant. in Concil., Constant. III.]

[49] [Cf. Crabbe, *Concilia*, I, 629.]

tains, and peers have had authority to subscribe in council, have not emperors and kings the like authority?

Truly there had been no need to handle so plain a matter as this is with so many words and so at length if we had not to do with those men who, for a desire they have to strive and to win the mastery, use of course to deny all things, be they never so clear, yea, the very same which they presently see and behold with their own eyes. The Emperor Justinian made a law to correct the behavior of the clergy and to cut short the insolent lewdness of the priests. And albeit he were a Christian and a catholic prince, yet put he down from their papal throne two Popes, Sylverius and Vigilius, notwithstanding they were Peter's successors and Christ's vicars.[50]

Let us see then, such men as have authority over the bishops, such men as receive from God commandments concerning religion, such as bring home again the ark of God, make holy hymns, oversee the priests, build the temple, make orations touching divine service, cleanse the temples, destroy the hill altars, burn the idols' groves, teach the priests their duty, write them out precepts how they should live, kill the wicked prophets, displace the high priests, call together the councils of bishops, sit together with the bishops, instructing them what they ought to do, condemn and punish an heretical bishop, be made acquainted with matters of religion, which subscribe and give sentence, and do all these things not by another man's commission but in their own name, and that both uprightly and godly. Shall we say it pertaineth not to such men to have to do with religion? Or shall we say, a Christian magistrate which dealeth amongst others in these matters doth either naughtily or presumptuously or wickedly? The most ancient and Christian emperors and kings that ever were did busy themselves with these matters, and yet were they never for this cause noted

[50] [Cf. *ibid.*, II, 1–3.]

either of wickedness or of presumption. And what is he that can find out either more catholic princes or more notable examples?

Wherefore, if it were lawful for them to do thus, being but civil magistrates and having the chief rule of commonweals, what offense have our princes at this day made which may not have leave to do the like, being in the like degree? Or what especial gift of learning, or of judgment, or of holiness have these men now that, contrary to the custom of all the ancient and catholic bishops, who used to confer with princes and peers concerning religion, they do now thus reject and cast off Christian princes from knowing of the cause and from their meetings?

Well, thus doing, they wisely and warily provide for themselves and for their kingdom, which otherwise they see is like shortly to come to nought. For if so be they whom God hath placed in greatest dignity did see and perceive these men's practices, how Christ's commandments be despised by them, how the light of the Gospel is darkened and quenched out by them, and how themselves also be subtly beguiled and mocked and unwares be deluded by them, and the way to the kingdom of heaven stopped up before them; no doubt they would never so quietly suffer themselves neither to be disdained after such a proud sort nor so despitefully to be scorned and abused by them. But now, through their own lack of understanding, and through their own blindness, these men have them fast yoked and in their danger.

We truly for our parts, as we have said, have done nothing in altering religion, either upon rashness or arrogancy, nor nothing but with good leisure and great consideration. Neither had we ever intended to do it except both the manifest and most assured will of God, opened to us in his Holy Scriptures, and the regard of our own salvation, had even constrained us thereunto. For, though we have departed from that church which these men call catholic, and by that means get us envy amongst them that want skill to judge, yet is this enough for us, and it ought to be enough for every wise and good man and one that maketh account of everlasting life, that we have gone from that church which had power to err, which Christ, who cannot err, told so long before it should err, and which we ourselves did evidently see with our eyes to have gone from the old holy fathers, and from the apostles, and from Christ his own self, and from the primitive and catholic church; and we are come, as near as we possibly could, to the church of the apostles and of the old catholic bishops and fathers, which church we know hath hitherunto been sound and perfect and, as Tertullian termeth it, a pure virgin, spotted as yet with no idolatry nor with any foul or shameful fault; and have directed according to their customs and ordinances not only our doctrine but also the sacraments and the form of common prayer.

And, as we know both Christ himself and all good men heretofore have done, we have called home again to the original and first foundation that religion which hath been foully neglected and utterly corrupted by these men. For we thought it meet thence to take the pattern of reforming religion from whence the ground of religion was first taken, because this one reason, as saith the most ancient father Tertullian, hath great force against all heresies: "Look whatsoever was first, that is true; and whatsoever is latter, that is corrupt." [51] Irenaeus oftentimes appealed to the oldest churches, which had been nearest to Christ's time, and which it was hard to believe had erred.[52] But why at this day is not the same common respect and consideration had? Why return we not to the pattern of the old churches? Why may not we hear at this time amongst us the same saying which was openly pronounced in times past in the council at Nicaea by so many bishops and catholic fathers, and nobody once speaking against it, ἔθη ἀρχαῖα κρατείτω: that is to

[51] [Tertullian, *Adversus Praxeam,* ch. ii.]
[52] [Irenaeus, *Contra haereses,* bk. III, ch. iii.]

say, "Hold still the old customs"? [53] When Esdras went about to repair the ruins of the temple of God, he sent not to Ephesus, although the most beautiful and gorgeous temple of Diana was there; and when he purposed to restore the sacrifices and ceremonies of God, he sent not to Rome, although peradventure he had heard in that place were the solemn sacrifices called Heccatombae, and other called Solitaurilia, Lectisternia, and Supplications, and Numa Pompilius' ceremonial books. He thought it enough for him to set before his eyes and to follow the pattern of the old temple, which Solomon at the beginning builded according as God had appointed him, and also those old customs and ceremonies which God himself had written out by special words for Moses.[54]

The prophet Haggai, after the temple was repaired again by Esdras, and the people might think they had a very just cause to rejoice on their own behalf for so great a benefit received of Almighty God, yet made he them all burst out in tears because that they which were yet alive and had seen the former building of the temple before the Babylonians destroyed it called to mind how far off it was yet from that beauty and excellency which it had in the old times past before.[55] For then indeed would they have thought the temple worthily repaired if it had answered to the ancient pattern and to the majesty of the first temple. Paul, because he would amend the abuse of the Lord's Supper which the Corinthians even then began to corrupt, he set before them Christ's institution to follow, saying; "I have delivered unto you that which I first received of the Lord." [56] And when Christ did confute the error of the Pharisees, "Ye must," saith he, "return to the first beginning; for from the beginning it was not thus." [57] And when he found great fault with the priests for their uncleanness of life and

[53] [Cf. *Concilia sacrosancta,* tom. II, col. 32, Concil. Nic., canon 6.]
[54] [Ezra 3:2, 10.] [55] [Hag. 2:3; Ezra 3:12.] [56] [I Cor. 11:23.]
[57] [Matt. 19:8.]

covetousness and would cleanse the temple from all evil abuses, "This house," saith he, "at the first beginning was a house of prayer," wherein all the people might devoutly and sincerely pray together; and so were your parts to use it now also at this day. For it was not builded to the end it should be a "den of thieves." Likewise all the good and commendable princes mentioned of the Scriptures were praised, specially by those words that they had walked in the ways of their father David. That is, because they had returned to the first and original foundation and had restored religion even to the perfection wherein David first left it.

And therefore, when we likewise saw all things were quite trodden under foot of these men, and that nothing remained in the temple of God but pitiful spoils and decays, we reckoned it the wisest and the safest way to set before our eyes those churches which we knew for a surety that they never had erred, nor never had private Mass, nor prayers in strange and barbarous language, nor this corrupting of sacraments and other toys.

And, forsomuch as our desire was to have the temple of the Lord restored anew, we would seek no other foundation than the same which we knew was long agone laid by the apostles, that is to wit, our Saviour Jesus Christ.

And forsomuch as we heard God himself speaking unto us in his word, and saw also the notable examples of the old and primitive church; again, how uncertain a matter it was to wait for a general council and that the success thereof would be much more uncertain; but specially, forsomuch as we were most ascertained of God's will and counted it a wickedness to be too careful and overcumbered about the judgments of mortal men; we could no longer stand taking advice with flesh and blood but rather thought good to do the same thing that both might rightly be done and hath also many a time been done, as well of good men as of many catholic bishops; that is, to remedy our own churches by a provincial synod. For thus know we the old fathers used to put matters in experience before they came to the public universal council. There remain yet at this day canons written in councils of free cities, as of Carthage under Cyprian, as of Ancyra, of Neocaesarea, and of Gangra, which is in Paphlagonia, as some think, before that the name of the general council at Nicaea was ever heard of. After this fashion in old time did they speedily meet with and cut short those heretics the Pelagians and the Donatists at home, with private disputation, without any general council. Thus also, when the Emperor Constantius evidently and earnestly took part with Auxentius, the bishop of the Arians' faction, Ambrose, the bishop of the Christians, appealed not unto a general council, where he saw no good could be done by reason of the Emperor's might and great labor, but appealed to his own clergy and people, that is to say, to a provincial synod. And thus it was decreed in the council at Nicaea that the bishops should assemble twice every year.[58] And in the council at Carthage it was decreed that the bishops should meet together in each of their provinces at least once in the year,[59] which was done, as saith the council at Chalcedon, of purpose that if any errors and abuses had happened to spring up anywhere, they might immediately at the first entry be destroyed [60] where they first begun. So likewise, when Secundus and Palladius rejected the Council of Aquila, because it was not a general and a common council, Ambrose, Bishop of Milan, made answer that no man ought to take it for a new or strange matter that the bishops of the west part of the world did call together synods and make private assemblies in their provinces; for that it was a thing before then used by the west bishops no few times, and by the

[58] [Cf. *Concilia sacrosancta,* tom. II, col. 32, Concil. Nic., canon 5.]
[59] [Cf. *ibid.,* col. 1167, Concil. Carthage III, ch. ii.]
[60] [Cf. *ibid.,* tom. IV, cols. 763,6, Concil. Calched., act xv, canon 19.]

bishops of Greece used oftentimes and commonly to be done.[61] And so Charles the Great, being Emperor, held a provincial council in Germany for putting away images, contrary to the second council at Nicaea. Neither, pardy,[62] even amongst us is this so very a strange and new a trade. For we have had ere now in England provincial synods and governed our churches by homemade laws. What should one say more? Of a truth, even those greatest councils, and where most assembly of people ever was (whereof these men use to make such an exceeding reckoning), compare them with all the churches which throughout the world acknowledge and profess the name of Christ, and what else, I pray you, can they seem to be but certain private councils of bishops and provincial synods? For admit peradventure Italy, France, Spain, England, Germany, Denmark, and Scotland meet together; if there want Asia, Greece, Armenia, Persia, Media, Mesopotamia, Egypt, Ethiopia, India, and Mauretania, in all which places there be both many Christian men and also bishops, how can any man, being in his right mind, think such a council to be a general council? Or, where so many parts of the world do lack, how can they truly say they have the consent of the whole world? Or what manner of council, ween you, was the same last at Trent? Or how might it be termed a general council when out of all Christian kingdoms and nations there came unto it but only forty bishops, and of those some so cunning that they might be thought meet to be sent home again to learn their grammar and so well learned that they had never studied divinity?

Whatsoever it be, the truth of the Gospel of Jesus Christ dependeth not upon councils nor, as St. Paul saith, upon mortal creatures' judgments.[63] And if they which ought to be careful

[61] [Cf. *ibid.*, tom. II, col. 980, Concil. Aquilei.]
[62] [I.e., verily.] [63] [I Cor. 4:3.]

for God's church will not be wise, but slack their duty and harden their hearts against God and his Christ, going on still to pervert the right ways of the Lord, God will stir up the very stones and make children and babes cunning, whereby there may ever be some to confute these men's lies. For God is able (not only without councils, but also, will the councils, nill the councils) to maintain and advance his own kingdom. "Full many be the thoughts of man's heart," saith Solomon, "but the counsel of the Lord abideth steadfast." "There is no wisdom, there is no knowledge, there is no counsel against the Lord." [64] "Things endure not," saith Hilary, "that be set up with men's workmanship; by another manner of means must the church of God be builded and preserved; for that church is grounded upon the foundation of the apostles and prophets and is holden fast together by one cornerstone, which is Christ Jesus." [65]

But marvelous notable, and to very good purpose for these days, be Jerome's words: "Whosoever," saith he, "the devil hath deceived and enticed to fall asleep, as it were, with the sweet and deathly enchantments of the mermaids, the sirens, those persons doth God's word awake up, saying unto them, 'Arise thou that sleepest; lift up thyself, and Christ shall give thee light.' Therefore at the coming of Christ, of God's word, of the ecclesiastical doctrine, and of the full destruction of Nineveh and of that most beautiful harlot, then shall the people, which heretofore had been cast in a trance under their masters, be raised up, and shall make haste to go to the mountains of the Scripture; and there shall they find hills, Moses, verily, and Joshua the son of Nun; other hills also, which are the prophets; and hills of the New Testament, which are the apostles and the evangelists. And when the people shall flee for succor to such hills and shall be exercised in the reading of those kind of mountains, though they find not one to teach them (for the

[64] [Prov. 19:21.]
[65] [Hilary of Poitiers, *Tractatus in CXXVI Psalmum,* sec. 8.]

harvest shall be great but the laborers few), yet shall the good desire of the people be well accepted in that they have gotten them to such hills, and the negligence of their masters shall be openly reproved."[66] These be Jerome's sayings, and that so plain as there needeth no interpreter. For they agree so just with the things we now see with our eyes have already come to pass that we may verily think he meant to foretell, as it were, by the spirit of prophecy, and to paint before our face the universal state of our time, the fall of the most gorgeous harlot Babylon, the repairing again of God's church, the blindness and sloth of the bishops, and the good will and forwardness of the people. For who is so blind that he seeth not these men to be masters, by whom the people, as saith Jerome, hath been led into error and lulled asleep? Or who seeth not Rome, that is their Nineveh, which sometime was painted with fairest colors but now, her visor being pulled off, is both better seen and less set by? Or who seeth not that good men, being awaked as it were out of their dead sleep at the light of the Gospel and at the voice of God, have resorted to the hills of the Scriptures, waiting not at all for the councils of such masters?

But by your favor, some will say, these things ought not to have been attempted without the Bishop of Rome's commandment, forsomuch as he only is the knot and band of Christian society. He only is that priest of Levi's order whom God signified in the Deuteronomy, from whom counsel in matters of weight and true judgment ought to be fetched; and whoso obeyeth not his judgment the same man ought to be killed in the sight of his brethren; and that no mortal creature hath authority to be judge over him, whatsoever he do; that Christ reigneth in heaven and he in earth; that he alone can do as much as Christ or God himself can do, because Christ and he have but one council house; that without him is no faith, no

[66] Hieron. in Naum. cap. 3. [Jerome, *Commentariorum in naum prophetorum,* ch. iii, vers. 18 seqq.]

hope, no church; and whoso goeth from him quite casteth away and renounceth his own salvation. Such talk have the canonists, the Pope's parasites, surely but with small discretion or soberness; for they could scant say more, at least they could not speak more highly, of Christ himself.

As for us, truly we have fallen from the Bishop of Rome upon no manner of worldly respect or commodity. And would to Christ he so behaved himself as this falling away needed not; but so the case stood that, unless we left him, we could not come to Christ. Neither will he now make any other league with us than such a one as Nahas, the King of the Ammonites, would have made in times past with them of the city of Jabes,[67] which was to put out the right eye of each one of the inhabitants. Even so will the Pope pluck from us the Holy Scripture, the Gospel of our salvation, and all the confidence which we have in Christ Jesus. And upon other condition can he not agree upon peace with us.

For whereas some use to make so great a vaunt that the Pope is only Peter's successor, as though thereby he carried the Holy Ghost in his bosom and cannot err, this is but a matter of nothing and a very trifling tale. God's grace is promised to a good mind and to one that feareth God, not unto sees and successions. "Riches," saith Jerome, "may make a bishop to be of more might than the rest; but all the bishops, whosoever they be, are the successors of the apostles." [68] If so be the place and consecrating only be sufficient, why then Manasseh succeeded David, and Caiaphas succeeded Aaron. And it hath been often seen that an idol hath been placed in the temple of God. In old time Archidamus the Lacedaemonian boasted much of himself how he came of the blood of Hercules, but one Nicostratus in this wise abated his pride: "Nay," quod he, "thou seemest not to descend from Hercules; for Hercules destroyed ill men, but thou makest good men evil." And when the Pharisees bragged

[67] 1 Regum. [I Samuel] 11[:2].

[68] [Jerome, *Epist. ad Euagrium.*]

of their lineage how they were of the kindred and blood of Abraham, "Ye," saith Christ, "seek to kill me, a man which have told you the truth as I heard it from God. Thus Abraham never did. Ye are of your father the devil and will needs obey his will." [69]

Yet notwithstanding, because we will grant somewhat to succession, tell us, has the Pope alone succeeded Peter? And wherein, I pray you? In what religion? In what office? In what piece of his life hath he succeeded him? What one thing (tell me) had Peter ever like unto the Pope, or the Pope like unto Peter? Except peradventure they will say thus: that Peter, when he was at Rome, never taught the Gospel, never fed the flock, took away the keys of the kingdom of heaven, hid the treasures of his Lord, sat him down only in his castle in St. John Lateran and pointed out with his finger all the places of purgatory and kinds of punishments, committing some poor souls to be tormented and other some again suddenly releasing thence at his own pleasure, taking money for so doing; or that he gave order to say private Masses in every corner; or that he mumbled up the holy service with a low voice and in an unknown language; or that he hanged up the sacrament in every temple and on every altar and carried the same about before him, whithersoever he went, upon an ambling jennet,[70] with lights and bells; or that he consecrated with his holy breath oil, wax, wool, bells, chalices, churches, and altars; or that he sold jubilees, graces, liberties, advowsons, preventions, first fruits, palls, the wearing of palls, bulls, indulgences, and pardons; or that he called himself by the name of the head of the church, the highest bishop, bishop of bishops, alone most holy; or that by usurping he took upon himself the right and authority over other folk's churches; or that he exempted himself from the power of any civil government; or that he maintained wars, set princes together at variance; or that he, sitting in his chair, with his triple crown

[69] [John 8:40, 41.] [70] [I.e., a small Spanish horse or ass.]

full of labels, with sumptuous and Persian-like gorgeousness, with his royal scepter, with his diadem of gold, and glittering with stones, was carried about, not upon palfrey, but upon the shoulders of noblemen. These things, no doubt, did Peter at Rome in times past, and left them in charge to his successors, as you would say, from hand to hand; for these things be nowadays done at Rome by the Popes, and be so done as though nothing else ought to be done.

Or contrariwise, peradventure they had rather say thus: that the Pope doth now all the same things which we know Peter did many a day ago; that is, that he runneth up and down into every country to preach the Gospel, not only openly abroad, but also privately from house to house; that he is diligent and applieth that business in season and out of season, in due time and out of due time; that he doth the part of an evangelist; that he fulfilleth the work and ministry of Christ; that he is the watchman of the house of Israel, receiveth answers and words at God's mouth, and, even as he receiveth them, so delivereth them over to the people; that he is the salt of the earth; that he is the light of the world; that he doth not feed his own self but his flock; that he doth not entangle himself with the worldly cares of his life; that he doth not use a sovereignty over the Lord's people; that he seeketh not to have other men minister to him but himself rather to minister unto others; that he taketh all bishops as his fellows and equals; that he is subject to princes, as to persons sent from God; that he giveth to Caesar that which is Caesar's; and that he, as the old Bishops of Rome did (without any question), calleth the Emperor his lord. Unless therefore the Popes do the like nowadays, as Peter did the things aforesaid, there is no cause at all why they should glory so of Peter's name and of his succession.

Much less cause have they to complain of our departing, and to call us again to be fellows and friends with them and to believe as they believe. Men say that one Cobilon, a Lacedaemonian, when he was sent ambassador to the King of the Persians to treat of a league and found by chance them of the court playing at dice, he returned straightway home again, leaving his message undone. And when he was asked why he did slack to do the things which he had received by public commission to do, he made answer he thought it should be a great reproach to his commonwealth to make a league with dicers. But if we should content ourselves to return to the Pope and his popish errors, and to make a covenant not only with dicers but also with men far more ungracious and wicked than any dicers be, besides that this should be a great blot to our good name, it should also be a very dangerous matter, both to kindle God's wrath against us and to clog and condemn our own souls forever. For of very truth we have departed from him whom we saw had blinded the whole world this many an hundred year. From him who too far presumptuously was wont to say he could not err and, whatsoever he did, no mortal man had power to condemn him, neither kings, nor emperors, nor the whole clergy, nor yet all the people in the world together, no, and though he should carry away with him to hell a thousand souls. From him who took upon him power to command not only men but even God's angels, to go, to return, to lead souls into purgatory, and to bring them back again when he list himself; whom Gregory said, without all doubt is the very forerunner and standard-bearer of Antichrist and hath utterly forsaken the catholic faith. From whom also those ringleaders of ours, who now with might and main resist the Gospel and the truth, which they know to be the truth, have or this departed every one of their own accord and good will, and would even now also gladly depart from him, if the note of inconstancy and shame and their own estimation among the people were not a let unto them. In conclusion, we have departed from him to whom we were not bound, and who had nothing to lay for himself but only I know not what virtue or power of the place where he dwelleth and a continuance of succession.

And as for us, we of all others most justly have left him. For our kings, yea, even they which with greatest reverence did follow and obey the authority and faith of the Bishops of Rome, have long since found and felt well enough the yoke and tyranny of the Pope's kingdom. For the Bishops of Rome took the crown off from the head of our King Henry the Second and compelled him to put aside all majesty and, like a mere private man, to come unto their legate with great submission and humility, so as all his subjects might laugh him to scorn. More than this, they caused bishops and monks and some part of the nobility to be in the field against our King John, and set all the people at liberty from their oath whereby they ought allegiance to their kind; and at last, wickedly and most abominably, they bereaved the same king, not only of his kingdom, but also of his life. Besides this, they excommunicated and cursed King Henry the Eighth, the most famous prince, and stirred up against him, sometime the Emperor, sometime the French king, and, as much as in them was, put in adventure our realm to have been a very prey and spoil. Yet were they but fools and mad to think that either so mighty a prince could be scared with bugs and rattles, or else that so noble and great a kingdom might so easily, even at one morsel, be devoured and swallowed up.

And yet, as though all this were too little, they would needs make all the realm tributary to them and exacted thence yearly most unjust and wrongful taxes. So dear cost us the friendship of the city of Rome. Wherefore, if they have gotten these things of us by extortion, through their fraud and subtle sleights, we see no reason why we may not pluck away the same from them again by lawful ways and just means. And if our kings in that darkness and blindness of former times gave them these things of their own accord and liberality, for religion sake, being moved with a certain opinion of their feigned holiness; now, when ignorance and error is spied out, may the kings their successors take them away again, seeing they have the same authority the kings their ancestors had before. For the gift is void except it be allowed by the will of the giver; and that cannot seem a perfect will which is dimmed and hindered by error.

# Recapitulation

THUS ye see, good Christian reader, how it is no new thing though at this day the religion of Christ be entertained with despites and checks, being but lately restored and as it were coming up again anew, forsomuch as the like hath chanced both to Christ himself and to his apostles; yet nevertheless, for fear ye may suffer yourself to be led amiss and seduced with those exclamations of our adversaries, we have declared at large unto you the very whole manner of our religion, what our faith is of God the Father, of his only Son Jesus Christ, of the Holy Ghost, of the church, of the sacraments, of the ministry, of the Scriptures, of ceremonies, and of every part of Christian belief. We have said that we abandon and detest, as plagues and poisons, all those old heresies which either the sacred Scriptures or the ancient councils have utterly condemned; that we call home again, as much as ever we can, the right discipline of the church, which our adversaries have quite brought into a poor and weak case; that we punish all licentiousness of life and unruliness of manners by the old and long-continued laws, and with as much sharpness as is convenient and lieth in our power; that we maintain still the state of kingdoms in the same condition and state of honor wherein we have found them, without any diminishing or alteration, reserving unto our princes their majesty and worldly preeminence, safe and without impairing, to our possible power; that we have so gotten ourselves away from that church which they had made a den of thieves, and wherein nothing was in good frame or once like to the church of God, and which themselves confessed had erred many ways, even as Lot in times past gat him out of Sodom, or Abraham out of Chaldee, not upon a desire of contention but by the warning of God himself; and that we have searched out of the Holy Bible, which we are sure cannot deceive, one sure form of religion, and have returned again unto the primitive church of the ancient fathers and apostles, that is to say, to the first ground and beginning of things, as unto the very foundations and headsprings of Christ's church. And in very troth we have not tarried for, in this matter, the authority or consent of the Trent council, wherein we saw nothing done uprightly nor by good order; where also everybody was sworn to the maintenance of one man; where our princes' ambassadors were condemned; where not one of our divines could be heard, and where parts-taking and ambition was openly and earnestly procured and wrought; but, as the holy fathers in former time, and as our predecessors have commonly done, we have restored our churches by a provincial convocation and have clean shaken off, as our duty was, the yoke and tyranny of the Bishop of Rome, to whom we were not bound, who also had no manner of thing like neither to Christ, nor to Peter, nor to an apostle, nor yet like to any bishop at all. Finally, we say that we agree amongst ourselves touching the whole judgment and chief substance of Christian religion, and with one mouth and with one spirit do worship God and the Father of our Lord Jesus Christ.

Wherefore, O Christian and godly reader, forsomuch as thou seest the reasons and causes both why we have restored religion and why we have forsaken these men, thou oughtest not to marvel though we have chosen to obey our Master Christ rather than men. Paul hath given us warning how we should not suffer ourselves to be carried away with such sundry learnings, and to fly their companies in especial which would sow debate and variances, clean contrary to the doctrine which they had received of Christ and the apostles. Long since have these men's crafts and treacheries decayed and vanished and fled away at the sight and light of the Gospel, even as the owl doth at the sunrising. And albeit their trumpery be built up and reared as high as the sky, yet even in a moment, and as it were of the own self, falleth it down again to the ground and cometh to nought. For you must not think that all these things have come to pass by chance or at adventure; it hath been God's pleasure that, against all men's wills well-nigh, the Gospel of Jesus Christ should be spread abroad throughout the whole world at these days. And therefore men, following God's commandment, have of their own free will resorted unto the doctrine of Jesus Christ.

And for our parts, truly we have sought hereby neither glory, nor wealth, nor pleasure, nor ease. For there is plenty of all these things with our adversaries. And when we were of their side we enjoyed such worldly commodities much more liberally and bountifully than we do now. Neither do we eschew concord and peace, but to have peace with man we will not be at war with God. "The name of peace is a sweet and pleasant thing," saith Hilary; but yet beware, saith he, "peace is one thing, and bondage is another." [1] For if it should be so, as they seek to have it, that Christ should be commanded to keep silence, that the truth of the Gospel should be betrayed, that horrible errors should be cloaked, that Christian men's eyes should be bleared, and that they might be suffered to conspire openly against God; this were not a peace, but a most ungodly covenant of servitude. "There is a peace," saith Nazianzene, "that is unprofitable; again, there is a discord," saith he, "that is profitable." [2] For we must conditionally desire peace, so far as is lawful be-

[1] [Hilary of Poitiers, *Contra Arianos, vel Auxentium,* sec. 1.]
[2] [Gregory of Nazianzus, *Oratio VI, de Pace,* sec. 20.]

fore God, and so far as we may conveniently: for otherwise Christ himself brought not peace into the world but a sword.[3] Wherefore, if the Pope will have us reconciled to him, his duty is first to be reconciled to God. "For from thence," saith Cyprian, "spring schisms and sects, because men seek not the head, and have not their recourse to the fountain of the Scriptures, and keep not the rules given by the heavenly Teacher."[4] "For," saith he, "that is not peace but war; neither is he joined unto the church which is severed from the Gospel."[5] As for these men, they use to make a merchandise of the name of peace. For that peace which they so fain would have is only a rest of idle bellies. They and we might easily be brought to atonement touching all these matters were it not that ambition, gluttony, and excess did let it. Hence cometh their whining: their heart is on their halfpenny. Out of doubt their clamors and stirs be to none other end but to maintain more shamefully and naughtily ill-gotten things.

Nowadays the pardoners complain of us, the dataries,[6] the Pope's collectors, the bawds, and other which take gain to be godliness and serve not Jesus Christ but their own bellies. Many a day ago, and in the old world, a wonderful great advantage grew hereby to these kind of people; but now they reckon all is loss unto them that Christ gaineth. The Pope himself maketh great complaint at this present that charity in people is waxen cold. And why so, trow ye? Forsooth, because his profits decay more and more. And for this cause doth he hale us into hatred all that ever he may, laying load upon us with despiteful railings and condemning us for heretics, to the end they that understand not the matter may think there be no worse men upon earth than we be. Notwithstanding, we in the mean season are never

[3] [Matt. 10:34.]

[4] [Cyprian, *De unitate ecclesiae; Epistola LXXIV, ad Pompeio.*]

[5] [Cyprian, *De lapsis.*]

[6] [The Datary was a papal officer through whom petitions to the Pope had to pass. His name is derived from the fact that he affixed the "Datum Romae" to papal bulls.]

the more ashamed for all this; neither ought we to be ashamed of the Gospel. For we set more by the glory of God than we do by the estimation of men. We are sure all is true that we teach, and we may not either go against our own conscience or bear any witness against God. For, if we deny any part of the Gospel of Jesus Christ before men, he on the other side will deny us before his Father.[7] And if there be any that will still be offended and cannot endure Christ's doctrine, such, say we, be blind and leaders of the blind. The truth nevertheless must be preached and preferred above all; and we must with patience wait for God's judgment. Let these folk in the meantime take good heed what they do, and let them be well advised of their own salvation and cease to hate and persecute the Gospel of the Son of God, for fear lest they feel him once a redresser and revenger of his own cause. God will not suffer himself to be made a mockingstock. The world espieth a good while agone what there is a-doing abroad. This flame, the more it is kept down, so much the more with greater force and strength does it break out and fly abroad. Their unfaithfulness shall not disappoint God's faithful promise. And if they shall refuse to lay away this their hardness of heart and to receive the Gospel of Christ, then shall publicans and sinners go before them into the kingdom of heaven.

God and the Father of our Lord Jesus Christ open the eyes of them all, that they may be able to see that blessed hope whereunto they have been called; so as we may altogether in one glorify him alone who is the true God, and also that same Jesus Christ whom he sent down to us from heaven; unto whom, with the Father, and the Holy Ghost, be given all honor and glory everlastingly. So be it.

THE END OF THE APOLOGY

OF THE CHURCH OF ENGLAND

[7] [Matt. 10:33.]

## *The manner how the Church of England is administered and governed*

THE Church of England is divided into two provinces: Canterbury and York.

The province of Canterbury hath

The archbishop of the same, who is primate of all England and metropolitan,

The bishop of London,

The bishop of

| | |
|---|---|
| Winchester | Exeter |
| Ely | Rochester |
| Chichester | Peterborough |
| Hereford | St. Davies |
| Salisbury | St. Asaph |
| Worcester | Llandaff |
| Lincoln | Bangor |
| Coventry and Lichfield | Oxford |
| Bath and Wells | Gloucester, and |
| Norwich | Bristow. |

The province of York hath

The archbishop of the same, who is also primate of England and metropolitan,

The bishop of Durham, Carlisle, and Chester.

Amongst us here in England no man is called or preferred to be a bishop except he have first been instituted a priest or minister and be well able to instruct the people in the Holy Scriptures.

Every one of the archbishops and bishops have their several cathedral churches, wherein the deans bear chief rule, being men specially chosen both for their learning and godliness, as near as may be.

These cathedral churches have also other dignities and canonries, whereunto be assigned no idle or unprofitable persons but such as either be preachers or professors of the sciences of good learning.

In the said cathedral churches, upon Sunday and festival days, the canons make ordinarily special sermons, whereunto duly resort the head officers of the cities and citizens; and upon the working days thrice in the week one of the canons doth read and expound some piece of Holy Scripture.

Also the said archbishops and bishops have under them their archdeacons, some two, some four, some six, according to the largeness of the diocese; the which archdeacons keep yearly two visitations, wherein they make diligent inquisition and search both of the doctrine and behavior as well of the ministers as of the people. They punish the offenders; and, if any errors in religion and heresies fortune to spring, they bring those and other weighty matters before the bishops themselves.

There is nothing read in our churches but the canonical Scriptures, which is done in such order as that the psalter is read over every month, the New Testament four times in the year, and the Old Testament once every year. And if the curate be judged of the bishop to be sufficiently seen in the Holy Scriptures, he doth withal make some exposition and exhortation unto godliness.

And forsomuch as our churches and universities have been wonderfully marred and so foully brought out of all fashion in time of papistry as there cannot be had learned pastors for every parish, there be prescribed unto the curates of meaner understanding certain homilies devised by learned men which do comprehend the principal points of Christian doctrine; as of original sin, of justification, of faith, of charity, and suchlike, for to be read by them unto the people.

As for common prayer, the lessons taken out of the Scriptures, the administering of the sacraments, and the residue of service done in the churches are every whit done in the vulgar tongue which all may understand.

## *Touching the Universities*

MOREOVER, this realm of England hath two universities, Cambridge and Oxford.

And the manner is not to live in these within houses that be inns or a receipt for common guests, as is the custom in some universities; but they live in colleges under most grave and severe discipline, even such as the famous learned man Erasmus of Roterodame, being here amongst us about forty years past, was bold to prefer before the very rules of the monks.

In Cambridge be fourteen colleges, these by name that follow:

Trinity College, founded by King Henry the Eighth
King's College
St. John's College
Christ's College
Queens' College
Jesus College
Benet College [1]
Pembroke College, or Pembroke Hall
Peter College, or Peterhouse

[1] Corpus Christi College.

Gunwell and Caius College or Hall [2]
One other Trinity College, or Trinity Hall
Clare College, or Clare Hall
St. Catherine's College, or Catherine Hall
Magdalene College.

In Oxford likewise there be colleges, some greater, some smaller, to the number of four-and-twenty, the names whereof be as followeth:

The Cathedral Church of Christ, wherein also is a great company of students
Magdalen College
New College
Merton College
All Souls College
Corpus Christi College
Lincoln College
Auriell College [3]
Queen's College
Baylie College, or Balliol College
St. John's College
Trinity College
Exeter College
Brasenose College
University College
Gloucester College
Broadgates Hall
Hart Hall
Magdalen Hall
Alborne Hall [4]
St. Mary's Hall
White Hall
New Inn
St. Edmund's Hall.

And, besides these colleges that be in the universities, this realm hath also certain collegiate churches, as Westminster, Windsor, Eton, and Winchester. The two last whereof do bring up and find a great number of young scholars, the which, after they be once perfect in the rules of grammar and of versifying and well entered in the principles of the Greek tongue and of rhetoric, are sent from thence unto the universities; as thus: out of Eton College they be sent unto the King's College at Cambridge and out of Winchester unto the New College at Oxford.

The colleges of both the universities be not only very fair

[2] Gonville and Caius College.
[3] Oriel College.
[4] St. Alban's Hall.

and goodly built, through the exceeding liberality of the kings in old time and of late days of bishops and noble men, but they be also endowed with marvelous large livings and revenues.

In Trinity College at Cambridge, and in Christ's College at Oxford, both which were founded by King Henry the Eighth of most famous memory, are at the least found four hundred scholars; and the like number well near is to be seen in certain other colleges, as in the King's College and St. John's College at Cambridge; in Magdalen College and New College of Oxford; besides the rest which we now pass over.

Every one of the colleges have their professors of the tongues and of the liberal sciences (as they call them), which do train up youth privately within their halls, to the end they may afterward be able to go forth thence into the common schools as to open disputation, as it were into plain battle, there to try themself.

In the common schools of both the universities there are found at the King's charge, and that very largely, five professors and readers, that is to say,

The Reader of Divinity
The Reader of the Civil Law
The Reader of Physic
The Reader of the Hebrew tongue, and
The Reader of the Greek tongue.

And for the other professors, as of philosophy, of logic, of rhetoric, and of the mathematicals, the universities themselves do allow stipends unto them. And these professors have the ruling of the disputations and other school exercises which be daily used in the common schools; amongst whom they that by the same disputations and exercises are thought to be come to any ripeness in knowledge are wont, according to the use in other universities, solemnly to take degrees, every one in the same science and faculty which he professeth.

We thought good to annex these things, to the end we might

confute and confound those that spread abroad rumors how that with us nothing is done in order and as ought to be done, that there is no religion at all, no ecclesiastical discipline observed, no regard had of the salvation of men's souls; but that all is done quite out of order and seditiously, that all antiquity is despised, that liberty is given to all sensuality and lewd lusts of folks, that the livings of the church be converted to profane and worldly uses: whereas in very truth we seek nothing else but that that God above all most good may have still his honor truly and purely reserved unto him, that the rule and way to everlasting salvation may be taken from out of his very word and not from men's fantasies, that the sacraments may be ministered not like a masquery or a stage play but religiously and reverently according to the rule prescribed unto us by Christ and after the example of the holy fathers which flourished in the primitive church; that that most holy and godly form of discipline which was commonly amongst them may be called home again; that the goods of the church may not be launched out among worldlings and idle persons but may be bestowed upon the godly ministers and pastors which take pain both in preaching and teaching; that there may from time to time arise up out of the universities learned and good ministers and others meet to serve the commonwealth; and finally, that all unclean and wicked life may be utterly abandoned and banished, as unworthy for the name of any Christian. And, albeit we are not as yet able to obtain this that we have said fully and perfectly (for this same stable, as one may rightly call it, of the Romish Augeas cannot so soon be thoroughly cleansed and rid from the long-grown filth and muck); nevertheless this is it whereunto we have regard; hither do we tend; to this mark do we direct our pain and travail, and that hitherto (through God his gracious favor) not without good success and plenteous increase; which thing may easily appear to everybody, if either we be compared with our own selves, in which manner of case we have been but few years since, or else be compared with our false accusers or rather our malicious slanderers.

The Lord defend his church, govern it with his Holy Spirit, and bless the same with all prosperous felicity.
Amen.

Imprinted at London in Paul's
churchyard, at the sign
of the brazen serpent,
by Reginald Wolf

ANNO DOMINI MDLXIIII

# Bibliography


Andrewes, Lancelot. *Opuscula quaedam posthuma.* Oxford, 1852.

Bayne, C. G. *Anglo-Roman Relations, 1558–1565.* (Oxford Historical and Literary Studies II.) Oxford, 1913.

*A briefe discourse against the outwarde apparell and ministring garmentes of the popishe church.* N.p., 1566.

*A Briefe Discourse of the Troubles Begun at Frankfort.* Ed. John Petheram. London, 1846.

*A briefe examination . . . of a certaine declaration lately put in print in the name and defence of certaine ministers in London refusying to weare the apparell prescribed by the lawes and orders of the Realme.* London, [1566?].

Byrne, M. St. C. "The Mother of Francis Bacon," *Blackwood's Magazine,* CCXXXVI (1934), 758–771.

*Calendar of State Papers, Foreign, 1558–1589.* London, 1863–1950.

*Calendar of State Papers, Spanish, Elizabeth, 1558–1603.* London, 1892–1899.

Calvin, John. *Certain homilies . . . with an Apologie of Robert Horne.* [Rome?], 1553.

Cardwell, Edward. *Documentary Annals of the Reformed Church of England.* 2 vols. Oxford, 1839–1844.

Churchson, John. *A brefe treatyse declarying what and where the Churche is, that it is Knowen, and whereby it is tryed and Knowen.* London, 1556.

Cornford, Margaret E. *Paul's Cross.* London, 1910.

*Corpus Scriptorum Ecclesiasticorum Latinorum.* Vienna, 1866– .

Cowell, H. J. *The Four Chained Books.* London, 1938.

*The declaracyon of the procedynge of a conference, begon at Westminster the laste of Marche, 1559.* London, [1559?].

Dorman, Thomas. *A proufe of certeyne articles in religion denied by M. Iuell, sett furth in defence of the Catholyke beleef therein.* Antwerp, 1564.

Dugmore, C. W. *The Mass and the English Reformers.* London, 1958.

Evans, Lewis. *A brieve Admonition unto the nowe made Ministers of Englande: Wherein is shewed some of the fruicte of this theyr late framed fayth.* Antwerp, 1565.

Farmiloe, J. E. M., and Nixseaman, R., eds. "Elizabethan Churchwardens' Accounts," *Bedfordshire Historical Record Society,* XXXIII (1953), 11.

Fuller, Thomas. *The Worthies of England.* Ed. John Freeman. London, 1952.

Gardiner, Stephen. *De Vera Obediencia, An Oration made in Latine . . . And nowe translated into english and Printed bi Michal Wood.* Rouen, 1553.

Gee, Henry. *The Elizabethan Clergy and the Settlement of Religion, 1558–1564.* Oxford, 1898.

Harding, Thomas. *An Answere to Maister Iuelles Chalenge.* Louvain, 1564.

——. *A Briefe Answere of . . . touching certaine untruthes, with which Maister Iohn Iuell charged him in his late Sermon at Paules Crosse the viii of Iuly. Anno. 1565.* Antwerp, 1565.

——. *A Confutation of a Booke intituled An Apologie of the Church of England.* Antwerp, 1565.

——. *A Detection of sundrie foule errours . . . touching Doctrine . . . uttered and practized by M. Iewel, in a Booke lately by him set foorth entituled, A Defence of the Apologie &c.* Louvain, 1568.

——. *A Reioindre to M. Iewels Replie.* Antwerp, 1566.

——. *A Reioindre to M. Iewels Replie against the Sacrifice of the Masse.* Louvain, 1567.

Hooker, Richard. *The Laws of Ecclesiastical Polity.* 2 vols. London, 1907.

Hughes, Philip. *The Reformation in England.* Vol. III. London, 1954.

Humphrey, Laurence. *Ioannis Iuelli Angli, Episcopi Sarisburiensis vita & mors.* London, 1573.

Jewel, John. *Apologia Ecclesiae Anglicanae.* London, 1562.

——. *An Apologie, or aunswer in defence of the Church of England, concerninge the state of Religion used in the same.* London, 1562.

——. *An Apologie or answere in defence of the Church of Englande with a briefe and plaine declaration of the true Religion professed and used in the same.* Trans. Lady Bacon. London, 1564.

——. *The Copie of a Sermon pronounced by the Byshop of Salisburie at Paules Crosse.* London, 1560.

——. *A Defence of the Apologie of the Churche of Englande.* London, 1567.

——. *A Defence of the Apologie of the Churche of Englande.* London, 1571.

——. *Epistola cuiusdam Angli, qua asseritur consensus verae religionis doctrinae & caeraemoniarum in Anglia, contra vanissimos quorundam cavillos, quibus eandem suis ad plebeculam contionibus impugnare conantur.* N.p., 1561.

——. *A Replie unto M. Hardinges Answeare.* London, 1566.

——. *A Sermon made in Latine in Oxenforde, in the raigne of King Edward the sixt.* London, [1586?].

——. *The true copies of the Letters betwene the reverend father in God Iohn Bisshop of Sarum and D. Cole.* London, 1560.

——. A *Viewe of a Seditious Bul.* London, 1582.

——. *Works.* London, 1609.

——. *Works.* Ed. J. Ayre. 4 vols. (Parker Society.) Cambridge, 1845–1850.

Kennedy, W. P. M. *Elizabethan Episcopal Administration.* 3 vols. London, 1924.

Knappen, M. M. *Tudor Puritanism.* Chicago, 1939.

Latimer, Hugh. *Certayn Godly Sermons . . . collected by Augustine Bernher.* London, 1562.

Le Bas, C. W. *The Life of Bishop Jewel.* London, 1835.

Lewis, C. S. *English Literature in the Sixteenth Century.* Oxford, 1954.

MacLure, Millar. *The Paul's Cross Sermon, 1534–1642.* Toronto, 1958.

Martiall, John. *A Treatyse of the Crosse.* Antwerp, 1564.
Meyer, Arnold O. *England and the Catholic Church under Queen Elizabeth.* London, 1916.
Neale, J. E. *Elizabeth I and Her Parliaments, 1559–1581.* London, 1953.
——. *England's Elizabeth.* Washington, 1958.
——. *Essays in Elizabethan History.* London, [1958].
Nowell, Alexander. *A Reproufe . . . of a booke entituled, A Proufe of Certayne Articles in Religion denied by M. Iuell, set furth by Thomas Dorman.* London, 1563.
Osorio, Jerome. *An Epistle . . . to the most excellent Princesse Elizabeth.* Trans. Richard Shacklock. Antwerp, 1565.
Parker, Matthew. *Correspondence, 1535–1575.* Ed. J. Bruce and T. T. Perowne. (Parker Society.) Cambridge, 1853.
*Patrologiae Cursus Completus: Series Graeca.* Ed. J. P. Migne. Paris, 1857–1866.
*Patrologiae Cursus Completus: Series Latina.* Ed. J. P. Migne. Paris, 1844–1864.
Pollen, John H. *The English Catholics in the Reign of Queen Elizabeth.* London, 1920.
Primus, John H. *The Vestments Controversy.* Kampen, 1960.
Rastell, John. *A Treatise intitled, Beware of M. Iewel.* Antwerp, 1566.
Read, Conyers. *Mr. Secretary Cecil and Queen Elizabeth.* London, 1955.
——. "William Cecil and Elizabethan Public Relations," in *Elizabethan Government and Society.* Ed. S. T. Bindoff, Joel Hurstfield, and C. H. Williams. London, 1961.
Southern, A. C. *Elizabethan Recusant Prose, 1559–1582.* London, [1950].
Southgate, W. M. *John Jewel and the Problem of Doctrinal Authority.* Cambridge, Mass., 1962.
——. "The Marian Exiles and the Influence of John Calvin," in *The Making of English History.* Ed. R. L. Schuyler and H. Ausubel. New York, [1952].
Strype, John. *Annals of the Reformation.* 4 vols. Oxford, 1820–1840.
——. *The Life and Acts of Matthew Parker.* 3 vols. Oxford, 1821.
Tavard, G. H. *Holy Writ or Holy Church.* New York, 1960.

*A Transcript of the Registers of the Company of Stationers of London, 1554–1640*. Ed. E. Arber. 5 vols. London and Birmingham, 1875–1894.

Veech, Thomas M. *Dr. Nicholas Sanders and the English Reformation*. Louvain, 1935.

Whitgift, John. *Works*. Ed. J. Ayre. 3 vols. (Parker Society.) Cambridge, 1852.

Whiting, M. B. "The learned and virtuous Lady Bacon," *Hibbert Journal*, XXIX (1931), 270–283.

*The Zurich Letters*. Ed. Hastings Robinson. 2 vols. (Parker Society.) Cambridge, 1842–1845.

Zwingli, Huldreich. *The Rekening and declaration of the faith and belief of Huldrik Zwingly bischoppe of Zuryk*. Zurich, 1543.

# Index

Ailly, Pierre D' (Petrus de Alliaco), 46
Allen, William, xxxix
Aloysius, Peter, 53
Ambrose of Milan, 19, 28, 30, 31, 33, 40, 41, 114, 124
Anabaptists, 42
Ancyra, Council of (ca. 314), 124
Andrewes, Lancelot, xliii
Angelus Carletus de Clavasio, 97n.
Antonius de Rosellis, *see* Rosellis, Antonius de
Apollonius, 88
Aquila (Aquileia), Council of (381), 124
Arcadio, Emperor, 111n.
Archidamus the Lacedaemonian, 128
Arians, 42, 67, 111, 124
Aristotle, 105
Asotus, Peter, 109
Athanasius, 84, 111, 112
Augustine of Hippo, 19, 23, 25, 30, 31, 33, 35, 36-37, 40, 44, 65n., 67n., 76, 84, 86n., 87-88, 114
Auxentius, 72n., 112, 124
Aylmer, John, xxiv

Bacon, Lady Ann, xxxviii, xlvi-xlvii, 3-5
Bacon, Anthony, xlvi
Bacon, Francis, xlvi
Bacon, Nicholas, xii, xiii, xlvi
Bacon, Roger, 73
Bancroft, Richard, xlii
Baptism, teaching concerning, 31; *see* Sacraments
Baptista of Mantua, *see* Spagnuoli, Baptista (of Mantua)
Basil, 30
Beringer of Tours, 46n.
Bernard of Clairvaux, 53, 73, 75
Bernher, Augustine, xxi-xxii
Beza, Theodore, xlvi
Bonaventura, 38n.
Boniface VIII, 59, 60n., 61n.
Bonner, Edmund, xxii
Bucer, Martin, xliv
Bullinger, Heinrich, xxiii, xxxvii

Caesarea, Council of, 111
Cajetan, Thomas de Vio, 45
Calfhill, James, xl
Caligula, 99
Callistus I, 32
Calvin, John, xvi n., xliv
Cambridge University, 141-142, 143
Camotensis, 107, 108n.
Campeggio, Lorenzo, 52
Canterbury, Archbishop of, *see* Parker, Matthew

# *Index*


Carthage, Council of, 89, 124
Cartwright, Thomas, xliii
Casus, John, 53, 54
Catholicon, 96
Cecil, William, x, xii, xiii-xiv, xvii, xxix, xxxii, xxxviii, xlvii
Celsus, 57, 84
Ceremonies, ix-x, xxx-xxxi; teaching concerning, 37, 94
Chalcedon, Council of (451), 48, 116, 118, 124
Charlemagne, 61, 125
Charles V, Emperor, 61
Cherius, Cosmus, 53
Childeric III, 61n.
Chrysostom, John, 27, 29, 30, 32n., 35, 40, 41, 44, 63n., 80, 82, 84, 87, 111, 114
Church: teaching concerning, 24, 63-76; and error, 95-98; *see* Church and State *and* Primitive Church
Church and State, 56-63, 113-120; *see* Prince, Godly
Churchson, John, xiv-xv
Clement V, 60n.
Clement VII, 61n.
Clement, John, 86
Cobilon and the dicers, 131
Cole, Henry, xx, xxviii
Collegiate churches, 142
Constantine, civil magistrate, 118
Constantine, Emperor, 44, 116, 118
Constantinople, Council of (381), 116
Constantinople, Third Council of (681), 118
Constantius, 50, 124
Cooke, Anthony, xlvi
Cooper, Thomas, xl
Cornelius, Bishop of Bitonto, 109n.
Cossa, Basassare, *see* John XXIII, Antipope
Councils: authority of, 103-112; called by magistrates, 123-125; *see also under place of meeting*
Cox, Richard, xxii, xxiv
Cranmer, Thomas, xviii, xx, xxviii, xlv
Cyprian, 24, 25, 35, 50, 84, 87, 105, 124, 137
Cyril of Alexandria, 30, 34, 112

Dandalus, Francis, 62
Declaration of Faith (1559), xxiv-xxv, xxxviii, xlv
Dering, Edward, xli
Diasius, Alphonsus, 53
Diasius, John, 53
Dietrich von Nieheim, *see* Theodoricus de Niem
Dionysius, 30
Dioscorus, 118
Donatists, 124
Dorman, Thomas, xv, xl
Durandus, William, 91n., 109n.

Ebion, 43, 67
Edward VI, xviii, xxi
Egidius, *see* Giles of Rome
Eliberis, Council of (ca. 305), 87
Elizabeth I, ix-xiii, xvi
Ephesus, Council of (431), 116
Epiphanius, 44, 67, 87
Eucharist, xx, xxiv, xliv; teaching concerning, 31-36, 40-41, 46-47, 92, 101; *see* Sacraments
Eusebius of Caesarea, 9n., 29n., 48n., 71, 80n., 84
Evans, Lewis, xvi-xvii

Faber Stapulensis, 29
Ferdinand I, Emperor, 117
Frederick I (Barbarossa), 62n.
Fulgentius, 23n.

Gangra in Paphlagonia, Council of, 89, 124
Gardiner, Stephen, xxi, 46n., 47n.
Gelasius, 32, 33, 40, 41, 90, 101
Gerson, Jean, xxviii, 73-74, 107n.
Giles of Rome (Aegidius Romanos), 69
God, doctrine concerning, 22
Gregory I, 26, 63n., 72
Gregory VII, 62
Gregory of Nazianzus, 29, 50, 104, 136

Grindal, Edmund, xii, xxiv
Gualter, Rudolph, xxvi, xxxvii
Guest, Edmund, xxiv

Hadrian VI, Pope, 74, 110
Harding, Thomas, x, xvi, xx, xxxix, 52n.; life, xl, xli
Henry II, King of England, 132
Henry IV, Emperor, 62
Henry VI, Emperor, 62
Henry VIII, King of England, xxi, xlv, 132
Henry of Luxemburg, 61
Heresy, 17-20, 40-44
Heskyns, Thomas, xxxix
Hilary of Poitiers, 72, 126, 136
Holy Spirit, doctrine of, 23-24
Hooker, Richard, xliii
Horne, Robert, xii, xiii, xvi, xxiv
Hosius, Stanislaus, 77-79, 109
Hostiensis, Henricus de Segusio, 108n.
Huldericus, Bishop of Augusta, 29
Humphrey, Laurence, xvii n.

Innocent III, 60n.
Irenaeus, 121n.

Jerome, 13, 16, 19, 24-25, 30, 44, 84, 87, 107, 117, 127, 128
Jesus Christ: doctrine concerning, 22-23; mediator, 38
Jewel, John:
- life to 1561, xvii-xxix
- writings
  - Challenge Sermon, xxvi-xxviii
  - *Epistola,* xxix-xxxi
  - *Apology,* xiii-xiv, xxv, xxix, xxxi-xxxii, xxxvii-xxxix; summary of, xxxiii-xxxvii; importance of, xlii-xliv; translation of, xlv-xlvi
  - *A Replie,* xli
  - *Defence of the Apologie,* xli-xlii

Joachim of Fiore, 75
John XXIII, Antipope, 107
John, Bishop of Constantinople, 72
John, King of England, 62, 132
John of Salisbury, 108n.
Julian, 57
Julius I, Pope, 89
Julius III, Pope, 16
Justification by faith, xvi; teaching concerning, 38-39
Justin Martyr, 48, 82
Justinian, Emperor, 89, 119
Juvenal, Bishop, 118

Lactantius, 9n.
Lateran, Fifth Council of, 92n.
Latimer, Hugh, xx, xxii n.
Leo I, Pope, 90
Liberius, Pope, 107
Libertines, 42
Lombard, Peter, 46
Luther, Martin, xv, xvi, 45, 57, 59
Lyra, Nicholas, 108

Mammotrectus, 96
Marcian, Emperor, 116
Marcion, 78
Marshall, Richard, xxii
Marsiglio of Padua, 75
Martiall, John, x, xxxix
Martinengo, Papal Nuncio, xi, xxix
Martinus Magistris, 51n.
Mary Tudor, xix, xx
Maurice, Emperor, 25
Maximinus, Emperor, 80
Maximus, Bishop of Jerusalem, 111-112
Mennonites, 42
Milan, Council of, 112
Ministry, teaching concerning, 24-30
Mohammedans, 67
Montanus, 78

Nazianzene, *see* Gregory of Nazianzus
Neocaesarea, Council of (314), 124
Nestorius, 67
Nettesheim, Heinrich Cornelius Agrippa von, 108n.
Nicaea, Council of (325), 34-35, 107, 116, 124

# Index


Nicaea, Council of (787), 125
Nicostratus, 128
Novatian, 80n.
Nowell, Alexander, xv, xxvii, xl

Occam, *see* William of Occam
Ochino, Bernardino, xlvi
Origen, 30, 33, 36, 40, 44, 84n., 87
Osorio, Jerome, xvi
Oxford University, 141-142, 143

Palladius, 124
Panormitanus, 29, 108n.
Papacy, xv; teaching concerning, 25-26; immorality and, 51-55, 72-76, 91-92, 106-109, 127-132
Paphnutius, 112
Parker, Matthew, xii, xiii, xxii, xxv, xxxii, xxxviii, xlii, xlv, xlvi, 3-5
Parkhurst, John, xviii, xlii
Paschal II, Pope, 106-107
Patropassians, 112
Paula, 117
Paulinus, Bishop of Trier, 112
*Pauperes a Lugduno,* 74
Pausanius, 97n.
Pelagians, 124
Petrarch, Francesco, 75
Phocas, Emperor, 25
Pighius, Albertus (Pighi, Albert), 45n., 52, 74n., 77n., 79, 86, 96, 110
Pipin, 61
Pius II (Aeneas Sylvius), 29-30, 110
Pius IV, xi, 15, 104
Platina, Bartolomeo, 30n., 74n.
Plautus, 94
Plutarch, 97n., 103n.
Pointz, Robert, xxxix
Poissy, Conference of, xxxii
Pole, Reginald, 110
Polycarp of Smyrna, 48-49
Porphyry, 57
Prierias, Sylvester, 95
Primitive Church, xxiv, xxviii, 17, 64-65, 68-69, 83-93, 99-100, 120-121, 134
Prince, Godly, teaching concerning, 63, 113-120; *see* Church and State

Quadra, de (Spanish Ambassador), xi-xiii

Rastell, John, xl
Resurrection, doctrine of, 39
Ridley, Nicholas, xx, xxviii
Rome, Council of, 88
Rosellis, Antonius de, 59n., 92n.
Rufinus, 13-14, 44, 112n., 117

Sabellicus, Marc Antonio, 62n.
Sacraments, xxiv; teaching concerning, 30-31, 92, 100; *see* Eucharist
Sampson, Thomas, x
Sanders, Nicholas, xxxix
Sandys, Edwin, xxiv
Savonarola, Girolamo, 75
Schwenkfeld, Caspar, and Schwenkfeldians, 42n., 77-79
Scory, John, xxiv
Scotists, 45
Scotus, John Duns, 45n., 46
Scripture, xv, xix, xxiv, xxviii, 16-20; teaching concerning, 30; and Church, 76-82, 100, 120, 134
Secundus, 43, 124
Shacklock, Richard, xvi n., xxxix
Sleidanus, Johannes, 53n., 74n.
Smith, Richard, xl, 46n.
Socrates, historian, 44, 88n., 112n., 118
Sozomen, 29, 50, 67n., 107n., 112n.
Spagnuoli, Baptista (of Mantua), 75
Stapleton, Thomas, xxxix
Steuchus, Augustinus, 59n.
Suetonius, 10n.
Sylverius, Pope, 119
Symmachus, 57
Syrmium, Council of, 111, 112

Tacitus, Cornelius, 8
Terence, 52
Tertullian, 7n., 9n., 18n., 27, 50, 55-56, 64n., 80-81, 98, 121

Thalasius, Bishop, 118
Theodoret, 33, 40, 67, 86, 111n., 117, 118n.
Theodoricus de Niem, 97n.
Theodoricus de Schismate, 97n.
Theodosius I, 116, 118
Theodosius II, 116
Theophilus, 44
Theophylact, 33, 80
Thomas Aquinas and Thomists, 45, 46
Throckmorton, Nicholas, x, xiii-xiv, xxix, xxxi-xxxii
Trent, Council of, xi, xiii, xxix, xxxvi-xxxvii, xxxviii, 15-16, 90-91, 106, 125, 135

Valla, Lorenzo, 75
Vermigli, Peter Martyr, ix, xviii, xxiii, xxvi, xxxvii, xl, xliv
Vestiarian Controversy, xliii
Victor, Pope, 61
Vigilius, Bishop of Thapsus, 23
Vigilius, Pope, 119
Visitation of 1559, xxv-xxvi

Waldgrave, Edward, xii
Warwick, Earl of, xlii
Westminster Disputation, xxiii-xxiv, xxv, xxviii, xxxviii
Wharton, Thomas, xii
Whitehead, David, xiv, xxiv
Whitgift, John, xliii
William of Occam, 46
Winchester, Bishop of, *see* Horne, Robert
Wolf, Reginald, xlvi
Wolfius, John, xxxviii
Wood, Michal, xxi

Zacharias, Pope, 61n.
Zosimus, Pope, 107
Zwingli, Huldreich, xxi, 45, 57, 59